monday morning™

BODYART:
SEASONAL HOLIDAYS

by Carol Hauswald and Alice Maskowski
illustrated by Susan Pinkerton

In memory of Bobbie,
who taught us the pioneer spirit

Publisher: Roberta Suid
Editor: Carol Whiteley
Design & Production: Susan Pinkerton
Cover Art: David Hale

On-line address: MMBooks@AOL.com

1-878279-96-3
Printed in the United States of America
987654321

CONTENTS

INTRODUCTION

A New Year decoration in which the outlines of a child's hands turn into Father Time's beard. Handprint-covered wrapping paper for Kwanzaa gifts. An April Fool's Day monkey, suitable for hugging, made from a child's hand and foot prints.

The pages that follow provide models and simple directions that will enable you and your children to produce these and scores of other special-day creations based on hands, fingers, feet, toes, and other body parts. You'll also find related bulletin boards, crafts, songs, action verses, games, and snacks that turn *BodyArt* into a whole-learning environment that fosters imagination and self-esteem.

Celebrating Celebrations

This multi-sensory approach to learning focuses on seven special-day units:

Sukkot. A joyous October holiday, Sukkot (SU-koth) celebrates the splendor of the harvest. In this unit, children will make projects that relate to the bounty of the earth, including a shoe box *sukkah,* or covered arbor, which traditionally provides shelter or a special place for families to share meals.

Kwanzaa. Kwanzaa (KWAHN-zah) is a week-long African-American celebration. In Swahili, this holiday means "the first." *BodyArt* activities in this unit include weaving placemats and other projects that will help children appreciate different cultures.

Ringing in the New Year. A bulletin board filled with balloons heralds the happy New Year's celebration, a time both of quiet reflection and noisy anticipation. Measurement plays an important part in this unit with projects that utilize copies of the children's

hands as clock hands and special "sands of time" that represent the old and new years.

Preparing for Passover. Hailed as one of the greatest yearly festivals of the Jewish religion, Passover focuses on the joy of freedom. It also is a reminder not to take freedom for granted. A "Passover Plates" bulletin board helps celebrate this time of year, with *BodyArt* veggies, fruit, and bittersweet herbs. This is a good unit in which to discuss nutrition.

Egging on Easter. Easter falls on the first Sunday following the first full moon on or after March 21. Since it occurs during the spring, the *BodyArt* activities reflect the growing season; children make flowers and carrot-nibbling bunnies, newborn chicks, and sweet bunny baskets that hold delicious candies and decorated eggs.

April Fool's Day. Celebrating this day doesn't involve taking part in pranks. It does involve lots of laughter. Children will giggle at "knock, knock" jokes, at themselves as they walk in big clown feet, and at the huggable monkeys that are favorite *BodyArt* projects. The unit also concentrates on the magical aspects of this special occasion by including directions for rabbits and scarves that pop out of magicians' hats.

Children's Day. Children's Day, which falls on the second Sunday in June, can be celebrated by people all the world over. The activities in this unit aim at promoting self-esteem and at showing children how very special they are.

Literature Links

Each unit of *BodyArt: Seasonal Holidays* includes a list of picture book read-alouds. These books will awaken and sustain children's interest in language and in the subject matter covered. The books are sensitively written, beautifully illustrated, and age-appropriate; they make wonderful springboards to the units. Many of the read-alouds tie directly to specific *BodyArt* projects. For example, after listening to *The Egg Tree* by Katherine Milhous, you and the children can make your own egg tree and hang fingerprint-decorated paper eggs on its branches.

The picture books may also be used as follow-ups to *BodyArt* activities. The stories will inspire creative drama, puppetry, spontaneous games, child-drawn picture books, movement songs, child-dictated stories, and more—activities that all contribute to whole-language learning.

All of the read-alouds listed are readily available through libraries and bookstores. Inexpensive paperback editions can often be purchased through children's book clubs. Two clubs that we use frequently are:

The Trumpet Club
666 Fifth Avenue
New York, NY 10103

Scholastic, Inc.
730 Broadway
New York, NY 10003

Another good source for books is:
Sundance Distributors and
    Publishers
P. O. Box 1326, Newton Road
Littleton, MA 01460

Materials for the *BodyArt* Projects

The projects in this book require common arts and crafts supplies that most preschool centers have on hand: nontoxic tempera or finger paints, crayons, washable markers, nontoxic glue, scissors, hole punches, poster board, construction paper, paper fasteners, and rolls of colored bulletin board paper. *Note:* When using tempera paint, mix with a small amount of Staflo starch. This makes the paint adhere better to paper and eliminates flaking; it also gives a nice sheen to the finish. You can make your own finger paint by using a 50-50 mixture of tempera paint and starch. This will cut down on your material costs substantially.

Whenever possible, we recommend the use of recycled materials—items such as paper towel rolls, egg cartons, plastic milk bottles, cardboard from cereal boxes, and wallpaper samples. Using recycled supplies will keep student projects inexpensive—and make them earth-friendly too!

Where Do You Go from *BodyArt: Seasonal Holidays?*

If you and your children enjoy the projects in this *BodyArt* book, you may also be interested in the five other books in the series that employ this creative approach to learning. *BodyArt: World Holidays* features special days in countries all over the globe. *BodyArt: Holidays U.S.A.* celebrates the earth, Native American tribes, children, leaders, explorers, and animals. *BodyArt: People* deals with families, feelings, friends, and community. *BodyArt: Nature* focuses on four-legged animals, birds, fish, insects, spiders, and seasons. And *BodyArt: Holidays* celebrates birthdays, Halloween and harvest time, Hanukkah and Christmas, and "I Love You Days." Together these body-based arts and crafts books form a solid curriculum with which you can involve your children in enjoyable learning all year long.

What Is BodyArt?

Like all activities that build self-esteem, *BodyArt* begins with the children. *BodyArt* projects are arts and crafts activities based on the young creator's hands, fingers, feet, toes, and other body parts. The outlines and shapes of these body parts are then enhanced with a wide variety of free or inexpensive crafts materials and transformed into special works of art.

But *BodyArt* projects are much more than simply coloring within the lines or filling in worksheets. Intricately woven into them are children's own imaginations and personal perceptions. When viewing a circle, adults see the shape; but a child who has just drawn a circle may see a hot air balloon, an iridescent bubble, or a turtle with its head and feet pulled in. *BodyArt* draws on young children's creativity, and allows children to make unique contributions to their own projects—because without their special bodies and minds, there would be no artwork. Final products, therefore, will be treasured for years as testaments to the children's talents and uniqueness.

The projects themselves are fun and easy to do. Colors are bright and brash, lines are big and bold, shapes are repeated over and over again. As the children work through the activities, they become involved in a magical world, one that's bursting with excitement and meaningful involvement and learning.

One of these types of learning is preparatory learning. The child learns how to cut with scissors, which is a prewriting skill. He or she also learns how to make marks on paper, which fosters eye-hand coordination.

Academic learning also takes place with *BodyArt* units. After a unit is completed, for example, children have a better notion about measurements and directions. Finally, each *BodyArt* unit is designed to be sensitive to the needs of gender, culture, and ecological considerations. And all *BodyArt* learning is child-friendly.

Activities are slanted toward children from preschool to grade 1. At the earliest developmental level, children will simply provide the necessary body part for tracing and cutting by the adult; they'll complete the project by decorating the shape. More advanced children can trace the shapes themselves and assist in the cutting, as well as decorate. Older children will be able to handle all the tasks on their own. But no matter how much of a project young artists do, their efforts will lead to increased confidence. Each "I did it" experience will motivate children to achieve at ever-higher levels of learning.

In a nutshell, *BodyArt:*

• uses language for real, meaningful purposes so that children are able to make sense of their world and their place in it;

• actively involves children through experiential, inductive, and democratic processes;

• recognizes the learning environment as a social community in which educational resources are found;

• incorporates a wide variety of tactile, kinesthetic, visual, and listening activities that reach all learning styles;

• is highly adaptable to the typical learner, as well as to gifted and talented and learning-challenged children.

SUKKOT, THE FEAST OF TABERNACLES

The ancient Hebrews celebrated Sukkot (SU-koth) as a festival of thanksgiving. Beginning on the 15th day of the Hebrew month of Tishai (October), Sukkot lasts nine days. It's a joyous time of year when parades are held and roadside stands are filled with fresh tomatoes, apples, and other delicious fruits and vegetables.

As you discuss this fun-filled holiday with children, you'll be teaching them about how the bounty of the earth is grown and harvested, and what some of it tastes like. There's also an opportunity to teach colors and numbers—the choices for learning are limitless!

Explain to children that the *sukkahs,* or tabernacles, associated with this holiday are an integral part of the yearly celebration. According to tradition, these temporary structures provided much-needed shelter for the Jewish people after their exodus from Egypt as they journeyed toward the Promised Land. Today many families eat their meals in a homemade *sukkah* during this important holiday. Depending on the weather, you may want to include an outdoor snacktime as part of your Sukkot activities. It's a great way to appreciate all the delicious food that comes from Mother Earth!

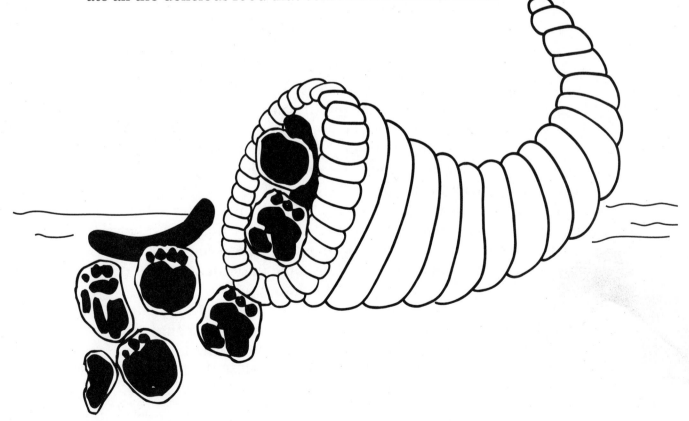

Happy Harvest Burlap Bulletin Board

This burlap board will help answer some of the questions children have about the way food grows.

Materials: One yard of 45"-wide natural burlap; squares of flannel (3 each of light green and dark green, 2 of brown, and 1 of yellow); scissors; safety pins or Velcro; white butcher paper; nontoxic, washable tempera (yellow, red, orange, purple, green, and blue); 6 disposable plastic plates; self-adhesive flannel or heavy masking tape; pencil

Directions: Cut a circle out of the yellow flannel for the sun. Attach it to the upper right-hand portion of the burlap with a safety pin or Velcro. Cut out three treetops from dark-green flannel and position them on the left-hand side of the burlap. Add brown flannel tree trunks. Cut the light-green flannel "grass" lengthwise in two and pin or Velcro each piece horizontally across the burlap (make sure there's enough room at the bottom for the ground). Pin on a dark-green bush on the grassy area.

Spread a large piece of white butcher paper on the floor for all the children to work on. Pour a small amount of tempera into each of the plastic plates and place the plates in the center of the paper. Move the plates toward the edges as the paper fills up with childrens' designs to prevent spills.

Now have the children dip their palms into the paint to create fruits and vegetables on the paper. In general, prints made from palms dipped in orange, red, purple, or green paint look like oranges, apples, plums, and lettuce, respectively. Prints made from finger tips dipped in orange and green paint look like carrots and beans, and those made with green and purple look like grapes. But children may make any fruits and vegetables they like. When all imprints have been made, the children should add finger tip "leaves" to appropriate produce.

When the fruits and veggies are dry, cut them out and attach them to the proper growing places on the burlap board with Velcro, self-adhesive flannel, or heavy-duty masking tape. Keep track of each child's creations by penciling his/her name underneath the appropriate imprints and including it in the cutout.

Note: For a more permanent burlap board, use fabric paint to attach flannel pieces on burlap. Roll up and store when finished. Safety pins and Velcro can be used when you place the flannel pieces in different configurations.

Shoe Box Sukkah

Building a backyard *sukkah* and decorating it with harvest fruits is one of the highlights of the year for many Jewish people. Our *sukkah* is covered with *BodyArt lulavs* (loo-LAWs), or date palms, and hanging citrus fruits called *etrogs* (et-ROWGs).

Materials: Green construction paper; crayon or pencil; scissors; shoe box; transparent tape; orange or red nontoxic, washable tempera; paint tray

Directions: Have an adult cut the shoe box. Flip it over so that the bottom is on top. Cut a large square piece out of each of the four sides, leaving enough support at the corners so that the shoe box can stand by itself. Leave the top of the box intact. To make the *lulavs,* trace the child's hand (fingers apart) on a piece of green construction paper six or seven times. Cut out the paper hands. To make *etrogs,* ask the child to dip his or her finger tips into the paint that has been poured into the shallow tray and make imprints on the *lulavs.* Let dry.

When thoroughly dry, position the *lulavs* on the roof and wall areas of the *sukkah.* Secure in place with transparent tape. Feel free to bend the *lulavs'* finger areas to give them a three-dimensional look.

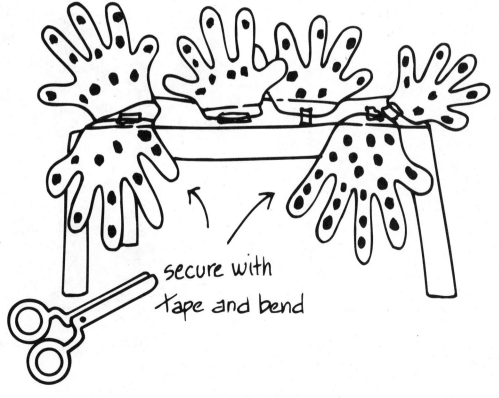

secure with tape and bend

Rose Mobile

Watching flowers grow from seed and then harvesting them is a wonderful treat for children. Here they group *BodyArt* flowers into a special garden.

Materials: Coat hanger; yarn; scissors; white paper; hole punch; red nontoxic, washable tempera; additional tempera colors (optional); paint tray

Directions: Ask the child to dip a hand (palm down, fingers apart) into a tray of red tempera paint and make an imprint on a piece of paper. Repeat the process on the same piece of paper, making imprints in a circle until a "sun-shaped" flower has been formed. Let the child make three "roses" for each mobile (using only red paint or other colors for a "garden variety").

After the paint dries, cut out each paper flower and punch a hole in the top. Loop a piece of yarn through the hole and tie to the coat hanger. Repeat for each flower using different lengths of yarn for a lovely flowering garden!

Horn of Plenty

In classical mythology, the cornucopia was a goat's horn containing an endless supply of food and drink. The Horn of Plenty has become a symbol of a good harvest season.

Materials: Horn of Plenty reproducible (p. 15); crayons; self-sealing plastic bag; scissors; transparent tape; nontoxic, washable paint; shallow paint trays

Directions: Copy, color, and cut out the reproducible. Make a vertical slit in the center of the horn's "mouth" and continue cutting away half of the mouth. Tape the small plastic bag to the back of the Horn of Plenty, making sure the opening is vertically aligned with the vertical edge of the Horn of Plenty's mouth. You should be able to reach your hand into the plastic bag through the cornucopia's mouth.

    To make fruits and vegetables, follow the directions in the "Happy Harvest Burlap Bulletin Board" activity (p. 8). Then have the children slip the "produce," one at a time, into the Horn of Plenty's mouth. There should be plenty of room in the plastic bag for all the child's "harvest."

Note: Don't be surprised if paper fruits and vegetables make numerous trips into and out of the cornucopia. Children love this activity because they get a chance to do just that! Take advantage of the opportunity to teach the concept of in and out, as well as counting, colors, and names of fruits and veggies. There's lots of learning in this fun activity.

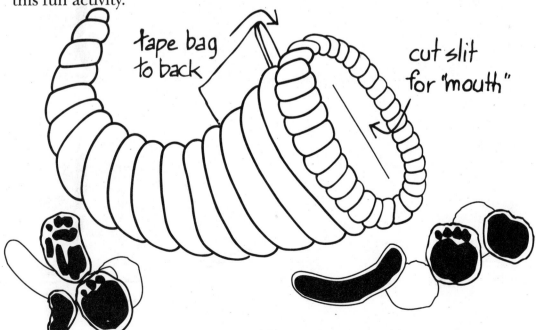

tape bag to back

cut slit for "mouth"

Sukkot Finger Plays and Movement Songs

Harvest Dance

(to the tune of "Here We Go 'Round the Mulberry Bush")

Here we go 'round the sukkah hut,
Sukkah hut, sukkah hut.
Here we go 'round the sukkah hut
So early in the morning!

Let's hang some oranges and pears,
Oranges and pears, oranges and
    pears.
Let's hang some oranges and pears
On our sukkah hut.

Let's hang our branches of palm,
Branches of palm, branches of palm.
Let's hang our branches of palm
On our sukkah hut.

The Growing Song

(to the tune of "This Old Man")

This little seed I plant in spring.
It will grow so big and strong.
With a knick-knack paddy-whack
Give the seed some sun.
This little seed will have some fun!

This bigger seed I water in summer.
It has tiny leaves that look like flowers!
With a knick-knack paddy-whack
Watch the seed grow tall
So we can harvest it in the fall!

This giant seed is ready to pick.
Get a spade and watch me dig.
With a knick-knack paddy-whack
Pull the carrot out.
That's what seeds are all about!

Say Hi to Pie Counting Song

(to the tune of "Ten Little Indians")

One little, two little, three little
    apples,
Four little, five little, six little
    apples,
Seven little, eight little, nine little
    apples,
Let's make apple pie!

(Substitute peach, pumpkin, and
other fruits to make up additional
delicious verses!)

Sukkot/Harvest Read-Alouds

Fiction

Baylor, Byrd. *The Way to Start a Day.* New York: Macmillan, 1978.

This Caldecott Honor book shows how Native Americans appreciate Earth's morning majesty.

Carle, Eric. *The Tiny Seed.* Saxonville, Mass.: Picture Book Studio, 1990.

Even though bigger seeds fly higher and sail farther on the wind, only the tiny seed becomes a flower in this beautifully illustrated picture book.

Cooney, Barbara. *Miss Rumphius.* New York: Viking, 1982.

The Lupine Lady used to be called Alice before she found her own way to make the world beautiful.

Marton, Jirina. *Flowers for Mom.* Ontario: Annick Press, 1991.

Jirka wants to bring his mom a big bouquet of flowers, but his kindness to others makes his mother cherish the gift all the more.

Romanova, Natalia. *Once There Was a Tree.* New York: Dial, 1983.

This beautifully illustrated picture book was first published in Russian. Its message: In nature, nothing goes to waste. Its story: An old tree split in two by lightning still has a purpose, especially for those tiny ticklers that make their homes in the tree's stump.

Spinelli, Eileen. *Thanksgiving at the Tappletons'.* New York: Lippincott, 1982.

Thanksgiving means turkey—or does it? This very special picture book spins an incredible story about a family that has to make do with less because of several mishaps. But the spirit of Thanksgiving is preserved in grand style.

Non-fiction

Allen, Marjorie N. and Shelley Rotner. *Changes.* New York: Macmillan, 1991.

Photographs of forests present vivid, realistic settings to teach children about changes that occur during the four seasons.

Anno, Mitsumasa. *Anno's Counting Book.* New York: Harper & Row, 1975.

The four seasons come alive in this delightful picture book, which also teaches numbers to children in a simple, effective way.

Burstein, Chaya. *Jewish Holidays and Traditions Coloring Book.* New York: Dover Publications, 1990.

A welcome addition for teaching young children about Hebrew holidays.

Caduto, Michael J. and Joseph Bruchac. *Keepers of the Earth.* Golden, Colo.: Fulcrum, 1989.

Native American legends and environmental activities for children are included in this rich resource.

Drucker, Malka. *A Jewish Holiday ABC*. San Diego: Harcourt Brace, 1989.
This wonderfully illustrated book helps children appreciate Judaism. Summaries for adults and a glossary are included.

Ehlert, Lois. *Eating the Alphabet*. San Diego: Harcourt Brace, 1989.
A favorite among children, with bright, primary colors and lots of learning included on every page. Also from the author: *Planting a Rainbow*, about how beautiful flowers grow from tiny seeds and bulbs; and *Growing Vegetable Soup*.

McMillan, Bruce. *Growing Colors*. New York: Lothrop, Lee & Shepard, 1988.
Photographs make the information in this picture book more realistic for young children. Colors correspond with fruits and vegetables so learning takes place on more than one level.

Moncure, Jane Belk. *My First Thanksgiving Book*. Chicago: Children's Press, 1984.
This easy-to-read offering tells about the Pilgrims and the Native Americans who helped them during the first harvest in Plymouth.

Prelutsky, Jack. *It's Thanksgiving*. New York: Scholastic, 1982.
From that cozy feeling at Grandmother's house to the Pilgrim's first Thanks-giving, Jack Prelutsky captures the full flavor of the "thankful" season.

Robinson, Fay. *Vegetables, Vegetables!* Chicago: Children's Press, 1994.
Photos make the information in this book especially real for young learners.

Ryder, Joanne. *Hello, Tree!* New York: Lodestar Books, 1991.
All children should have a special tree that's made just for them.

Slate, Elizabeth. *Nelly's Garden*. New York: Tambourine Books, 1991.
What wondrous things grow in Nelly's garden! This book is a pot-pourri of delightful information for children.

Titherington, Jeanne. *Pumpkin, Pumpkin*. New York: Scholastic, 1986.
How a pumpkin grows from seed is detailed in this wonderfully illustrated picture book.

Tresselt, Alvin. *Autumn Harvest*. New York: Mulberry Books, 1951.
City kids may not know that apples don't grow at the local supermarket. This book describes all that's required for a harvest each year.

Whitehead, Pat. *Best Thanksgiving Book*. Mahwah, New Jersey: Troll, 1985.
An A-B-C Thanksgiving book that's very easy for young children to understand.

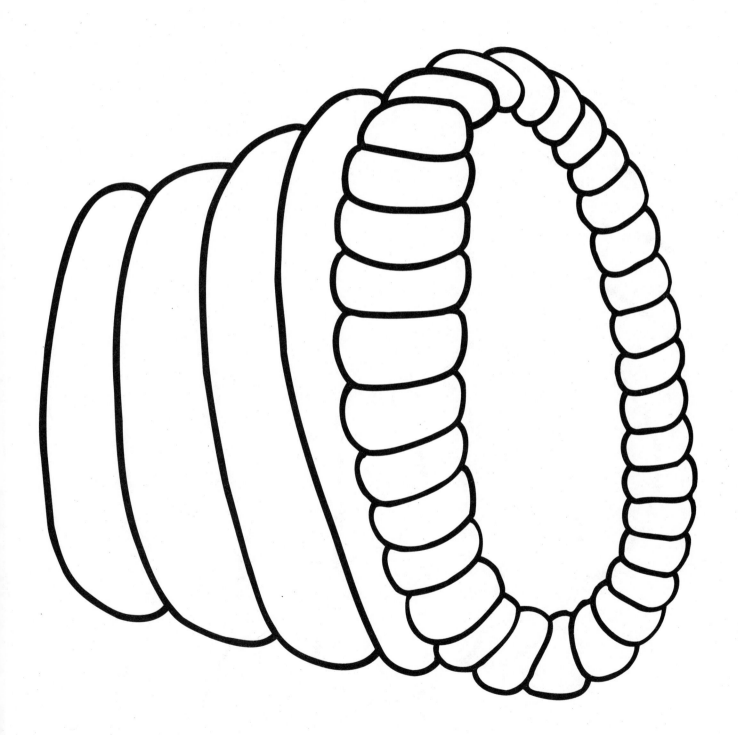

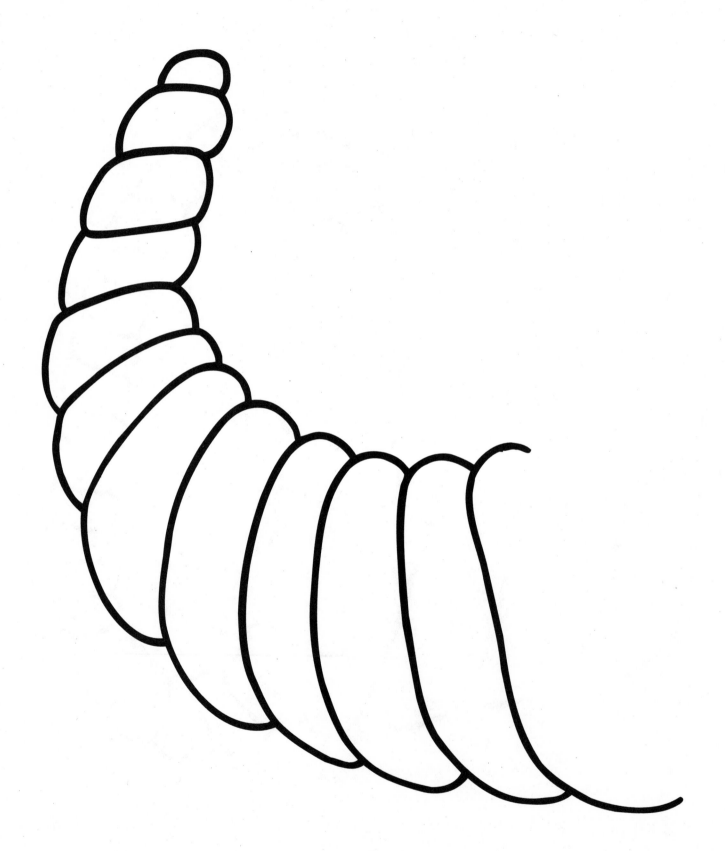

KWANZAA

Between Christmas and New Year's Day, African Americans celebrate a very special holiday called Kwanzaa (KWAHN-zah). The holiday was set aside for African Americans to learn about their history. In Swahili, Kwanza, or Yakwanza, means "the first." It stands for the first fruits of the harvest.

Kwanzaa lasts for seven days. During that time, children especially learn the *nguzo saba*, or seven principles: unity, self-determination, collective work and responsibility, cooperative economics, purpose, creativity, and faith.

Children of all races, colors, and creeds will enjoy learning about Kwanzaa. The *BodyArt* projects such as special-occasion wrapping paper and making a *kinara*, or candleholder for a Kwanzaa dinner table, will help teach about this important time. Children will be able to celebrate their differences, as well as their common bond as young people.

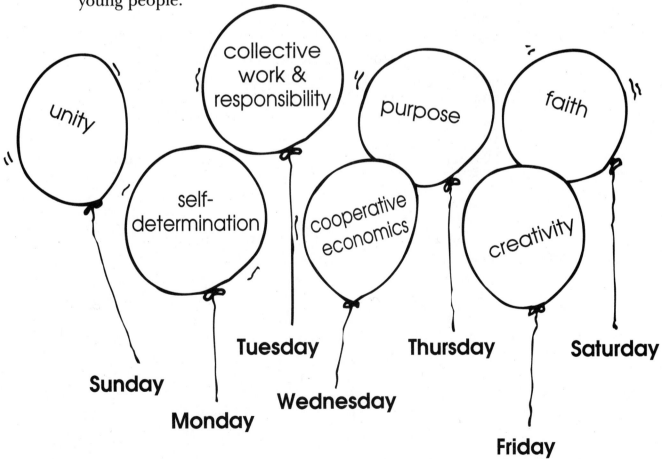

Kwanzaa Yenu Iwe Na Heri
(May Your Kwanzaa Be Happy)
Bulletin Board

Display the seven principles of Kwanzaa and discuss one on each day of the week-long celebration.

Materials: *Kinara* reproducible (p. 26); large sheet of white poster board; brown marker or crayon; black marker; construction paper (black, green, and red); scissors; glue; yellow nontoxic, washable tempera; shallow paint tray; transparent tape

Directions: Enlarge the reproducible on a copier. Position the *kinara* on the left-hand side of the poster board (leave a 12" column on the right-hand side). Color the *kinara* brown. Glue on 1" wide x 3" long strips of construction paper for candles: one black in the center, three red on the right, and three green on the left. On each of seven 12" wide by 2" deep strips of construction paper, print one of the following Kwanzaa words and its *BodyArt* translation:

   • Umoja (oo-MO-jah): "We are friends here." (This relates to the principle of unity.)
   • Kujichagulia (koo-jee-cha-goo-LEE-ah): "We make good choices." (This relates to the principle of self-determination.)
   • Ujima (oo-JEE-mah): "We work together." (This relates to the principle of collective work and responsibility.)
   • Ujamaa (oo-JAH-mah): "We share toys." (This relates to the principle of cooperative economics.)
   • Nia (NEE-ah): "We are important." (This relates to the principle of purpose.)
   • Kuumba (koo-OOM-bah): "We make good things." (This relates to the principle of creativity.)
   • Imani (ee-MAH-nee): "We are loved, protected, and cared for." (This relates to the principle of faith.)

On the first day of Kwanzaa, "light" the black candle by dipping a finger tip into yellow tempera and making a dot above it. Tack up the first idea strip. Talk to the children about the concept and try to apply it during the day. Glue the strip to the top right of the board at the end of the day. Repeat the process with the other ideas, alternating "lighting" red and green candles.

Kinara

The *kinara* (kee-NAH-rah), or candleholder, is often referred to as the heart of a Kwanzaa table setting. The seven candles it holds are called the *mishumaa saba* and represent the seven principles of Kwanzaa.

Materials: *Kinara* reproducible (p. 26); crayons or markers (brown, green, red); scissors; shallow paint tray; yellow nontoxic, washable tempera

Directions: Copy the reproducible and color it brown. Color the three candles on the right red, and the three on the left green. Cut out the *kinara*. Each day of Kwanzaa, the child can "light" one candle by dipping a finger tip in yellow paint and making a dot directly above it ("light" the brown candle first, then the red candle closest to the center, the green candle closest to the center, and so on). The *kinara* can be taken home at the end of the week.

Note: Keep the yellow tempera on the thick side; even undiluted, yellow paint can be runny. Mix first to get the consistency you want.

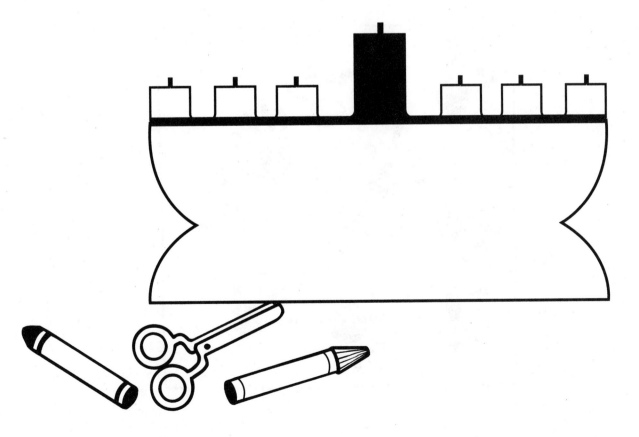

Zawadi Wrapping Paper

Zawadi (zah-WAH-dee) are gifts that are given to children on the sixth day of Kwanzaa. Homemade gifts are encouraged because they coincide with the sixth principle of Kwanzaa—*kuumba* (koo-OOM-bah), or creativity. This paper is great for wrapping up special classmate or family presents.

Materials: White tissue paper; black, red, and green nontoxic, washable tempera; shallow paint trays; transparent tape; bows and ribbons (optional)

Directions: Fill the paint trays with the tempera. Spread out a sheet of white tissue paper. Ask the child to dip a hand into one of the paint trays and make three or four imprints on the tissue paper. Finger tip "dot" imprints may be added for variety. Repeat the process with the other colors until the entire sheet is filled with green, red, and black prints. After the paper has dried completely, it may be used to wrap drawings or other gifts. Add bows or ribbon ties if desired.

Note: Hands should be washed between dips in different-colored paint to avoid "muddy" imprints.

Mkeka

The *mkeka* (mm-KEH-kah), or placemat, is important during the Kwanzaa celebration. Often made of handwoven straw, it stands for history or the past. The *BodyArt mkeka* will become historic too as a reminder to parents of how wonderful their child's hands are.

Materials: 12" x 18" brown construction paper; 9" x 12" construction paper in a variety of skin tones; thin strips of red, black, and green construction paper; scissors; craft knife; pencil or marker; clear, self-adhesive plastic; glue

Directions: Trace both of the child's hands on a sheet of skin-tone construction paper. Cut out. Then cut 1/4" wide x 6" long strips of black, red, and green construction paper (three or four of each color). In each paper palm area, cut 1/4" wide vertical slits with the craft knife in several rows, leaving a 1/4" margin between the woven area, the heel, and the base of the fingers.

Next, weave alternate-colored paper strips through the slits of one hand. Trim off the edges. Repeat for the second hand. When the weaving is finished, glue the hands to a large sheet of brown construction paper. Laminate with clear plastic for durability.

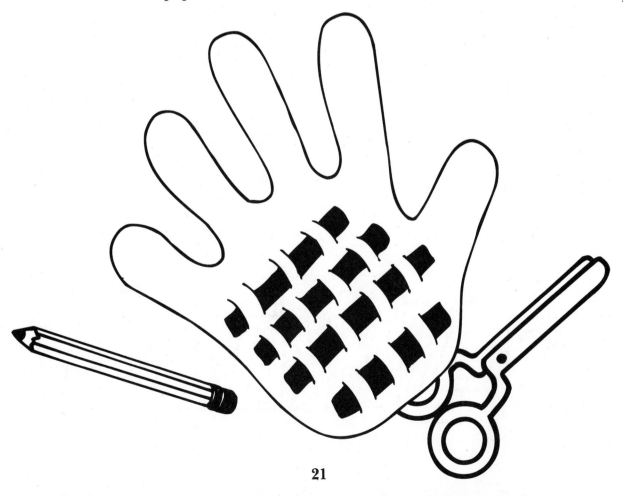

Kwanzaa Finger Plays and Movement Songs

Kwanzaa Learning Verse

(This learning verse helps children remember what Kwanzaa is all about.)

Today is the first day of Kwanzaa.
Light the black candle of unity.
Umoja (oo-MO-jah).
We are friends here.
Umoja.

Today is the second day of Kwanzaa.
Light the red candle of self-determi-
    nation.
Kujichagulia (koo-jee-cha-goo-LEE-
    ah).
We make good choices.
Kujichagulia.

Today is the third day of Kwanzaa.
Light the green candle of collective
    work and responsibility.
Ujima (oo-JEE-mah).
We work together.
Ujima.

Today is the fourth day of Kwanzaa.
Light the red candle of cooperative
    economics.
Ujamaa (oo-JAH-mah).
We share toys.
Ujamaa.

Today is the fifth day of Kwanzaa.
Light the green candle of purpose.
Nia (NEE-ah).
We are important.
Nia.

Today is the sixth day of Kwanzaa.
Light the red candle of creativity.
Kuumba (koo-OOM-bah).
We make good things.
Kuumba.

Today is the seventh day of
    Kwanzaa.
Light the green candle of faith.
Imani (ee-MAH-nee).
We are loved, protected, and cared
    for.
Imani.

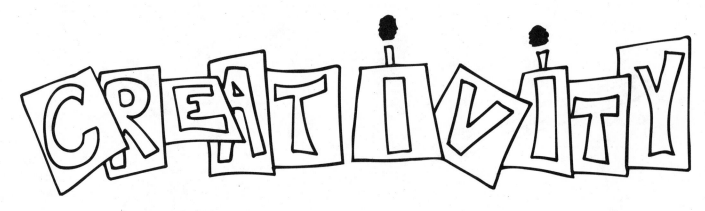

Kwanzaa Read-Alouds

Fiction

Aardema, Verna. *Bimwili & the Zimwi.* New York: Dial, 1985.

Little sister Bimwili finds, then loses, a shell by the sea. When she goes back to reclaim it, an ugly Zimwi traps her and turns her into a singing drum. Later, her sisters discover Bimwili in the drum and play a trick on the mean, old Zimwi.

Aardema, Verna. *Bringing the Rain to Kapiti Plain.* New York: Dial, 1981.

This beautifully illustrated picture book tells a Nandi tale that was featured on "Reading Rainbow." In the story the plains suffer from the lack of rain. Only a little boy named Kipat can end the terrible drought.

Burden-Patmon, Denise. *Imani's Gift at Kwanzaa.* Cleveland, Ohio: Modern Curriculum Press, 1992.

Grandmother (M'dear) and Imani share a special African-American holiday, which Imani learns about as Grandmother braids Imani's hair. A glossary helps readers understand and appreciate Kwanzaa.

Dillon, Diane and Leo. *Honey, I Love and Other Love Poems.* New York: Crowell, 1972.

Wonderfully sensitive poems that children of all ages like. African-American children will especially relate to the everyday experiences shared by the Dillons.

Flournoy, Valerie. *The Patchwork Quilt.* New York: Dial, 1985.

Tanya learns from her grandmother that a good quilt is like a masterpiece. It takes a long time to make one well.

Hoffman, Mary and Caroline Bind. *Amazing Grace.* New York: Scholastic, 1991.

Grace can do most anything she sets her mind to do.

Hudson, Cheryl Willis and Bernette G. Ford. *Bright Eyes, Brown Skin.* Littleton, Mass.: Sundance, 1990.

This primary offering illustrated by George Ford can boost self-esteem for African-American children.

Keats, Ezra Jack. *Apt. 3.* London: Hamish Hamilton, 1971.

This "Reading Rainbow" book features the relationship between Sam and his harmonica-playing neighbor.

Keats, Ezra Jack. *The Snowy Day.* New York: Viking, 1962.

This Caldecott Medal winner is a classic story of fun on a snowy day as experienced by a playful African-American child.

Polacco, Patricia. *Chicken Sunday.* New York: Scholastic, 1992.

Easter is coming and Miss Eula sees a pink hat in the window. Her grandchildren want to buy it for her.

Steptoe, John. *Mufaro's Beautiful Daughters*. New York: Scholastic, 1987.

Beautifully illustrated and honored as a Caldecott winner, this Cinderella story is taken from a South African folk tale. It tells of two beautiful daughters—one kind, the other mean-spirited. Kindness wins the day.

Sullivan, Charles. *Children of Promise*. New York: Harry N. Abrams, 1991.

The title of this collection of African-American literature and art is taken from Galatians 4:28, which says, "Now we, brethren, as Isaac was, are the children of promise." Especially designed for young people, it's a treasure worthy of a place in your permanent library collection.

Nonfiction

Aliki. *A Weed Is a Flower*. New York: Simon & Schuster, 1988.

The life of George Washington Carver comes alive in Aliki's picture book, telling how Carver's peanut research brought new life to the economy of the South.

Chocolate, Deborah M. Newton. *Kwanzaa*. Chicago: Children's Press, 1990.

In this book, children can learn about the meaning of Kwanzaa and how it is celebrated. Beautifully illustrated by Melodye Rosales.

Feelings, Muriel. *Moja Means One*. New York: Dial, 1971.

This fine Caldecott Honor Book introduces readers to the countries where Swahili is spoken. Wonderful soft-focus illustrations by Tom Feelings.

Marzollo, Jean. *Happy Birthday, Martin Luther King*. New York: Scholastic, 1993.

A picture book biography beautifully illustrated by Brian Pinkney. The story tells how Dr. King sought to make changes through peace, not violence.

Musgrove, Margaret. *Ashanti to Zulu*. New York: Dial, 1976.

Newcomers will learn about African traditions from A to Z in this Caldecott Medal winner with illustrations by Leo and Diane Dillon. You'll need more than one reading time to complete this enriching offering.

Kwanzaa Snacktime

Kwanzaa Creations

According to Kwanzaa tradition, ears of corn (*vibunzi* or *muhindi*) represent the number of children in a family. One ear of corn is placed on the *mkeka*, or special placemat, for each child. Since corn is an important part of the week-long Kwanzaa celebration, make and serve cornbread, accompanied by applesauce, for a special snack treat.

Another yummy treat during Kwanzaa is peanut butter, in sandwich form. Peanut butter can be served in honor of the famous African-American scientist George Washington Carver. Children can learn about Carver in the book *A Weed Is a Flower* by Aliki. Accompany sandwiches with crisp red apples.

Kwanzaa Game

The Lion Sleeps Tonight!

In the jungle, the mighty jungle, the lion sleeps tonight. . . . Maybe, maybe not! In this hide-and-seek game your learning center is transformed into a tropical forest and each child is a lion or lioness. The lions' jobs are to find "prey"

(stuffed animals or pictures of animals) that are hidden in the room.

To put the children in a jungle mood, hang green crepe paper around the room. Or have an adult use face paint to draw a lion face on each consenting child. Hypoallergenic face cream will take off the paint.

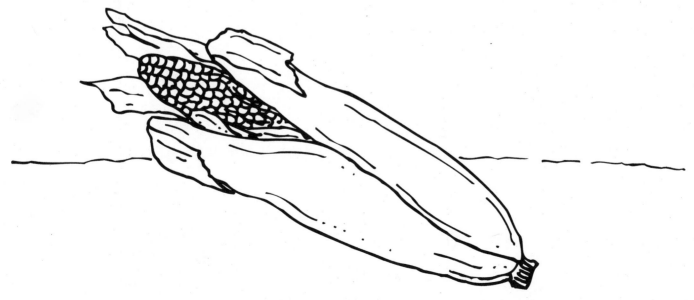

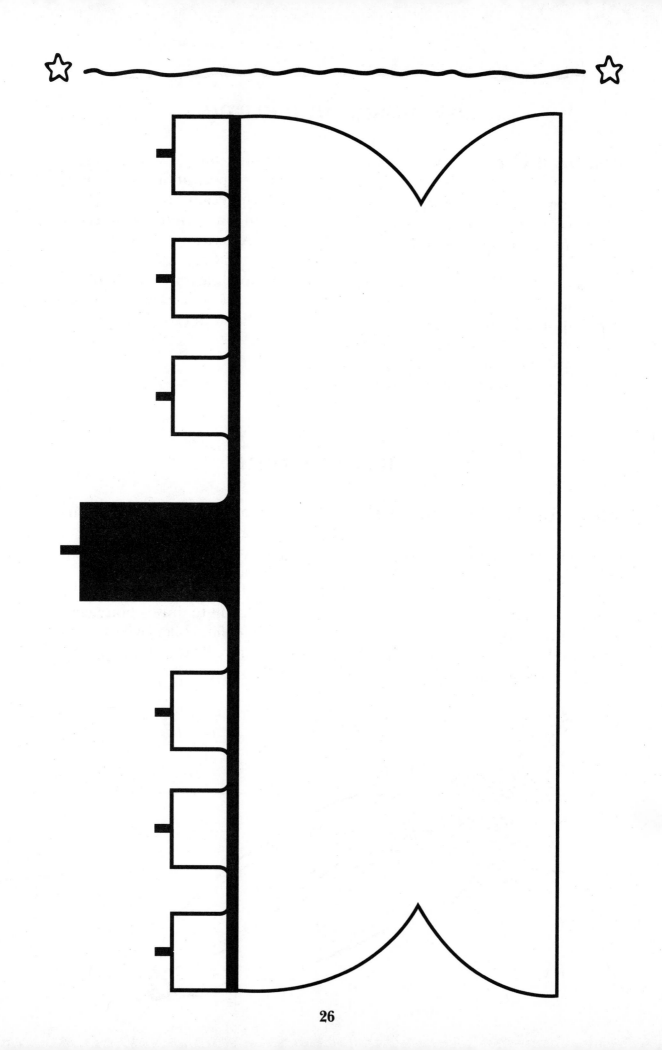

RINGING IN THE NEW YEAR

No other holiday focuses on the elements of time the way New Year's does. Every year, wherever they live—city, country, or suburbs—families and friends gather together to say goodbye to the past year and hello to the one that's about to begin. It's a quiet time of reflection and calmness, as well as a noisy time of renewal and excitement.

BodyArt projects in this unit, such as the "Hello/Goodbye Silhouette," help children think about time in new ways. They also show that every goodbye can be a hello waiting to happen!

Good-Bye, Old Year, Hello, New Year Bulletin Board

What better way to say goodbye to one year and welcome to another than with balloons! These *BodyArt* balloons also represent childrens' smiling faces.

Materials: Large poster boards, balloons (six per poster board), marker, photographs of the children (optional), tape, glue, construction paper (in multicultural skin-tone colors), scissors

Directions: Make as many bulletin boards as you need so that there is a representative balloon for each child in the group. After blowing up the balloons, draw a face on each with a marker (or glue on a photograph of each child). Tape two rows of three balloons on each poster board, leaving approximately four inches between balloons.

Next, trace each child's left hand (fingers apart) and forearm onto a piece of construction paper. Then trace each child's right hand and forearm. Cut out the paper hands and arms. Tape or glue a right arm and a left arm to either side of each balloon to make it look like the balloon people are waving—goodbye to the old year with one hand and hello to the new year with the other.

Option: To liven up the board even more, bunch up the paper arms a bit between glued or taped portions. This adds a three-dimensional look, a technique that can be used on other bulletin board and student projects.

Hello/Goodbye Silhouette

The first month of the year gets its name from Janus, the ancient Roman god of gates and doorways. Janus is usually depicted with two faces looking in opposite directions—an appropriate way to say goodbye to one year and hello to the next!

Materials: Three colors of 12" x 18" construction paper, scissors, light source, nontoxic glue, masking tape, colored pencil, chair, wall surface, photos of the child (optional), magazines for cutting out pictures

Directions: Tape a large piece of construction paper to a wall. Position the child on a chair close to the wall so that a light source focused on him or her will project a shadow image onto the paper. Trace the child's profile with a colored pencil (light or dark, depending on the paper color you are using) and cut out. Cut out a second profile on a different colored sheet of construction paper using the first one as a guide. Glue one profile facing left to the left side of a third piece of construction paper. Glue the second profile facing right to the right side of the paper.

If a photo of the child is available, glue it to the silhouette facing left; add photos of the child engaged in activities from the past year, if available. Cut out and glue on pleasant scenes from a magazine to the silhouette facing right to represent enjoyable activities in the year to come.

Father Time/Baby Time

This "flip-around" project is a great way to show children that the end of one year means the beginning of a new one. In it, the old man's beard becomes the new baby's hair. The resulting project can be used in games as well as movement songs.

Materials: Large paper plate, paper fastener, markers or crayons (gray, tan or brown, blue, pink, yellow, black), scissors, white construction paper, hole punch, pencil

Directions: To make Father Time, color the outside border of the paper plate gray to represent gray hair. Add gray eyebrows, a leathery tan or brown face, wise brown or gray eyes, and a distinguished nose. Trace the child's hand (fingers apart) onto a sheet of white construction paper twice. Color one side of both paper hands gray to represent Father Time's beard.

To make the New Year's baby, flip the paper plate over and upside down. Draw a large blue or pink outline of a baby's face in the center of the plate. Add large blue eyes, a wide mouth, and a button nose. Turn over the paper hands that were painted gray for Father Time and color the backs brown, yellow, or black to represent the New Year's baby's hair.

Now cut out the two double-colored paper hands. Punch a hole in the bottom of each palm area. Then punch a hole in the paper plate; the hole should fall in the center of the baby's scalp as well as under the nose of Father Time. Position one paper hand, gray side forward and with fingers pointing down, to be Father Time's beard; turn the plate over and position the second paper hand, brown (or yellow or black) side forward with fingers pointing up, to be the baby's hair. When everything is in place, insert a paper fastener through both hands and the plate and secure.

punch holes and attach beard and hair →

Sands of Time

Time is measured as sand passes through an hourglass, but in this hourglass children can capture time and make it stand still.

Materials: Plain or colored sand; 12" x 18" black construction paper; nontoxic, washable glue; brush; white crayon or chalk

Directions: Outline the child's left hand (fingers together) with white crayon or chalk on the bottom portion of a sheet of black construction paper. Then turn the paper around and trace the child's left hand again (fingers together) so that the fingertips of the two tracings meet. To add sand to the hourglass shape, brush glue around the edge and then spread more glue on the inside. Sprinkle sand over the hourglass and let dry.

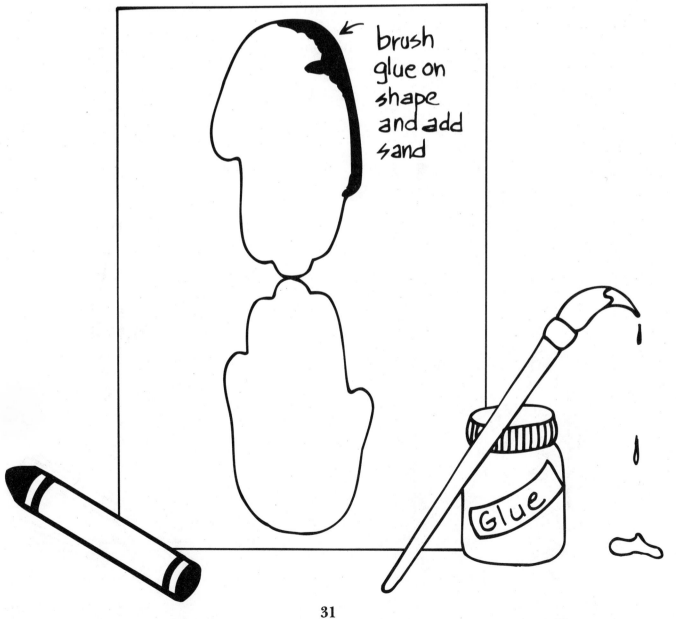

brush glue on shape and add sand

"Hand-some" Clock

The children's hands become hour and minute hands on the face of a special clock.

Materials: Clock reproducible (p. 36); poster board; clear laminating paper; construction paper (two colors of your choice); paper fastener; scissors; nontoxic, washable glue; pencil; hole punch

Directions: Copy, cut out, and glue the clock reproducible onto a piece of poster board. Cover with clear laminating paper for durability. To make the hour hand, ask the child to position his or her hand so that the pointing (index) finger is up and the rest of the fingers and thumb are hidden. Trace the hand in this position onto construction paper and cut out. To make the minute hand, repeat the process using different colored construction paper and adding more length to the index finger tracing. Finally, punch a hole in the center of the clock as well as in the bottom palm area of both paper hands. Insert a paper fastener through the holes and secure to the back of the clock.

New Year Finger Plays and Movement Songs

Father Time/Baby Song

(to the tune of "The Farmer in the Dell"—the children can hold up their "Father Time/Baby Time" plates [p. 30] as they sing)

The baby says hello,
The baby says hello.
The baby is the new year
And the baby says hello!

The baby smiles wide,
The baby smiles wide.
It'll be a good year
So the baby smiles wide!

The old year says goodbye,
The old year says goodbye.
The old man is the old year
And he says goodbye!

The old man smiles too,
The old man smiles too.
It's been a good year
So the old man smiles too!

The New Year Song

(to the tune of "Hickory Dickory Dock")

Hickory dickory dock,
December runs down the clock!
January appears, we welcome the
    year,
Hickory dickory dock!

New Year Cheer!

Let's cheer the old year!
(Children make cheering noises.)
Let's wave goodbye!
(Children wave goodbye.)
Here comes the new year!
(Children look excited.)
Let's say "Hi!" (Children wave
    hello.)

New Year Read-Alouds

Fiction

Cassidy, Clara. *We Like Kindergarten.* New York: A Golden Book, 1965.

Carol goes to kindergarten and learns how to make friends. Your preschoolers will enjoy hearing about what it's like to begin a "new year" in kindergarten.

Gilman, Phoebe. *Something from Nothing.* New York: Scholastic, 1992.

This beautifully illustrated story tells of a Jewish grandfather who makes a blanket for his baby grandson. In time, the blanket wears out, but instead of throwing it away Grandpa makes a jacket out of it. He continues to make smaller and smaller items to wear until the reader thinks a lost button is the last of it. But the grown-up grandson finds yet another way to make something from nothing.

Lesser, Carolyn. *The Goodnight Circle.* San Diego: Harcourt, 1984.

The story begins in the forest at the end of the day with a mother deer and her fawn. It ends with their morning search for food. The sense of the continuity in nature is portrayed.

Plath, Sylvia. *The Bed Book.* New York: Harper & Row, 1976.

Every child instinctively understands that the end of the day is like the end of a year. In this humorous account by a well-known poet, beds come in all sizes—not just tucked-in-tight nighty-night beds!

Shulevitz, Uri. *Dawn.* Toronto: Sunburst, 1974.

Lovely watercolor illustrations capture in a wonderfully poetic way the passing of time.

Viorst, Judith. *The Good-Bye Book.* New York: Macmillan, 1992.

A little boy tries everything he can think of to keep his mom from getting a baby sitter and going out without him. When the baby sitter arrives, however, the boy finds out it isn't so bad.

Williams, Margery. *The Velveteen Rabbit.* New York: Holt, 1983.

This classic read-to tale is a must for your library. Wonderfully illustrated, the story teaches how even toys have a history—as well as a chance for a new beginning.

Nonfiction

Barrs, Tony. *Clocks.* New York: Grosset & Dunlap, 1973.

Children learn all the different ways to tell time with clocks.

Klein, Leonore. *Just a Minute—a Book About Time.* New York: Harvey House, 1969.

How many times have kids heard parents say "Just a minute"–and vice versa! In this offering, children find out exactly how long time is.

Scarry, Richard. *All Year Long.* New York: Golden Press, 1976.

Bedtime, morning, night, seasons, and months are delightfully detailed.

New Year Snacktime

Good Luck Snacks

There are many foods that are associated with luck for the new year, such as black-eyed peas.

Festive-looking foods will also be a hit. Set out bowls of multi-colored spiral-shaped pasta and serve plain or with margarine, red sauce, or sprinkles of cheese.

New Year Game

Who Am I?

This guessing game utilizes the "Father Time/Baby Time" paper plate (p. 30). Start the game by making a statement to the children such as, "Sometimes I cry when I'm hungry." Then ask, "Who am I?" The children should turn their paper plate to the appropriate side. Continue making statements about either the baby or Father Time and have children react accordingly. After a while children may want to take turns making the statements themselves. This learning game is a good way to introduce comparing and contrasting skills.

"I've lived many years. Who am I?"

PREPARING FOR PASSOVER

Passover is one of the most important celebrations of the Jewish religion. It begins on the 14th day of the Jewish month of Nisan (late March or early April) and lasts for eight days. Passover is celebrated in memory of the time when Moses led the Hebrew slaves out of Egypt and into the Sinai Desert. Freedom is the great gift that this holiday celebrates each year.

Of special importance during Passover is the *Seder,* a special dinner during which the story of the slaves' exodus is told. *Seders,* which are eaten on the first and second nights of Passover, include foods that symbolize the bitterness of being slaves and the sweetness of new life as a free people.

Because food is an important part of Passover, and because the unit includes food-related projects, such as *BodyArt* silverware and *Seder* dishes, this is a good unit in which to teach children how eating a balanced meal will help them stay healthy—just as it kept the Jewish people healthy when they lived in the desert for 40 years some 3,500 years ago. Since cleaning and preparation are also a part of Passover, this is a good time to teach and practice both hygiene and organizational skills.

Passover Plates Bulletin Board

Make your own *Seder* meal and use it to teach cultural concepts and nutrition.

Materials: Large poster board; 2 sheets of self-adhesive Contac paper; paper plates; pencil or marker; construction paper (green, orange, brown, red, white); scissors; glue; stapler (optional); non-toxic, washable tempera paint (brown, purple, red); paint trays; white paper; glass of salt water

Directions: Cover the poster board with a "tablecloth" of two sheets of self-adhesive Contac paper. Then make each of the paper plate foods described below and glue or staple to the board.

Karpas—Represented here by *BodyArt* lettuce (or parsley), *karpas* are the first greens of spring. Trace the child's hand (fingers apart) on a sheet of green construction paper three times. Cut out the paper hands. Glue with fingers pointing up to a paper plate.

Maror, or bittersweet herbs—Trace the child's hand (fingers apart) onto a sheet of orange construction paper. Have the child dip his or her fingers into brown and red paint and make dots on the paper hand. Cut out when dry and glue to a paper plate.

Haroset—This sweet apple-and-nut-based spread is represented here by apples and nuts. Cut out two apple and several nut shapes from red and brown construction paper, respectively. Trace four of the child's fingers on green construction paper and cut out. Glue two finger "leaves" to each apple. Glue apples and nuts to a paper plate.

Grapes—Have the child dip his or her fingers into purple tempera and make grape imprints on a sheet of white paper. Cut out in a bunch shape. Trace the child's hand twice (fingers apart) on green construction paper and cut out for grape leaves. Glue to the top of the grape prints. Glue the grapes to a paper plate.

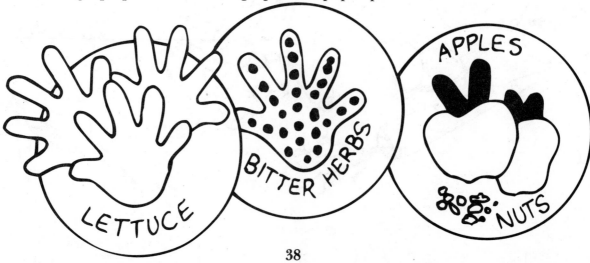

Sea of Reeds

One of the most interesting Passover legends tells about how the waters of the Sea of Reeds parted so that Moses could lead his people through them.

Materials: Blue and green construction paper, scissors, wooden craft stick, white poster board, transparent tape, crayons or markers, pencil, glue

Directions: To make the Sea of Reeds, trace both of the child's hands (fingers apart) on a sheet of blue construction paper. Cut out the paper hands. Bend the paper fingers forward so they extend up and in. Cut a 1/2" wide by 5" long slit in the center of the shorter length of a 12" x 18" piece of green construction paper. Glue a paper hand, palm up, to each side of this slit.

To make Moses and his followers, trace the child's hand (fingers together) on a piece of white poster board. Draw faces and long robes on the fingers and palm. Cut out the hand and glue a wooden craft stick to its back. Slip the stick through the slit in the "sea" and move it back and forth to recreate Moses's incredible journey!

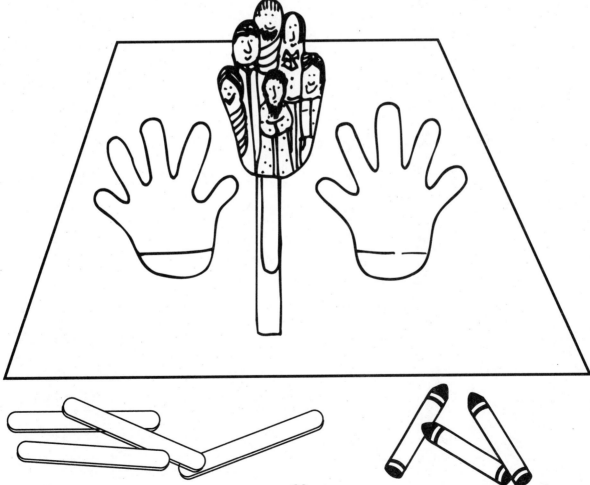

Passover Silverware

Whether you're teaching about Passover or nutrition, children will love to have their own knife, fork, and spoon. They can use them to pretend to eat and in games and movement songs.

Materials: Aluminum foil or white self-adhesive plastic paper, scissors, poster board or cardboard, masking tape or nontoxic glue, pencil or marker

Directions: To make the silverware, trace the child's hand and arm up to the elbow onto poster board or cardboard three times. For the fork, the fingers are apart; for the spoon, the hand is in a fist; and for the knife, the fingers are together. Cut out the three different "utensils." Wrap aluminum foil or self-adhesive paper around each shape. If foil is used, roll several small pieces of masking tape and place them between the foil and the cardboard where the foil ends meet. Press the foil to the cardboard. Or adhere the foil with glue.

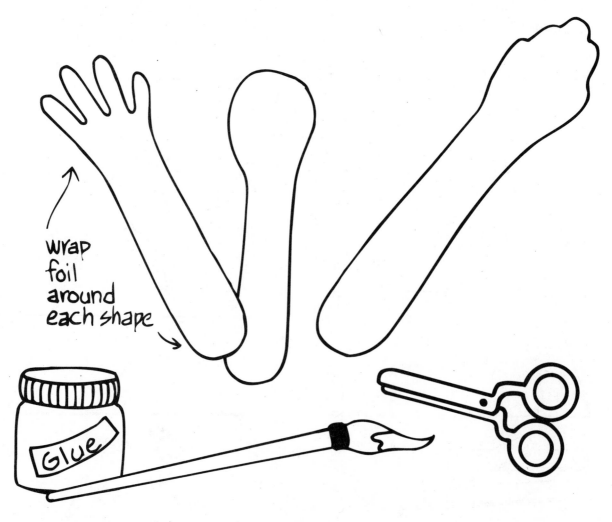

wrap foil around each shape

Passover Finger Plays and Movement Songs

The Cleaning Song

(to the tune of "This Is the Way We Wash Our Clothes"—let the children make appropriate motions)

This is the way we clean our rooms,
Clean our rooms, clean our rooms.
This is the way we clean our rooms
To prepare for Passover.

This is the way we pick up toys,
Pick up toys, pick up toys.
This is the way we pick up toys
To prepare for Passover.

This is the way we sweep the floor,
Sweep the floor, sweep the floor.
This is the way we sweep the floor
To prepare for Passover.

This is the way we wash the windows,
Wash the windows, wash the windows.
This is the way we wash the windows
To prepare for Passover.

(Let the children pick their favorite activity for a final stanza.)

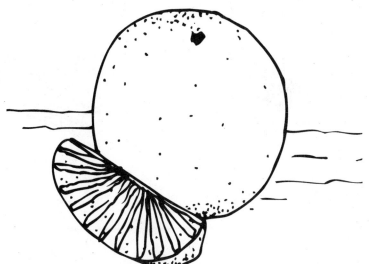

Festive Food Finger Play

(Acted out while sitting down, this activity uses the face as well as the fingers. It also helps reinforce color identification.)

I'm going to eat something pink.
It's called watermelon!
(Show a color picture of watermelon; let the children make eating motions.)

I'm going to eat something yellow.
It's called sweet corn!
(Show a color picture of corn; let the children make eating motions.)

I'm going to eat something green.
It's called seedless grapes!
(Show a color picture of grapes; let the children make eating motions.)

I'm going to eat something red.
It's called a juicy apple!
(Show a color picture of an apple; let the children make eating motions.)

I'm going to eat something orange.
And it's called an orange!
(Show a color picture of an orange; let the children make eating motions.)

Passover Read-Alouds

Fiction

Polacco, Patricia. *Mrs. Katz and Tush.* New York: Dell, 1992.

This "Reading Rainbow" featured book celebrates Passover as well as the special relationship between Mrs. Katz, an old Polish woman, and Tush, an African-American child.

Nonfiction

Adler, David. *A Picture Book of Jewish Holidays.* New York: Holiday House, 1981.

Passover is one of several Jewish holidays included in this beautifully illustrated, easy-to-read children's book.

Burstein, Chaya. *Jewish Holidays and Traditions Coloring Book.* New York: Dover, 1990.

This primary-age offering explains the important Jewish holidays—all of which grew out of events or periods in Israel's history.

Silverman, Maida. *Festival of Freedom: The Story of Passover.* New York: Simon & Schuster, 1988.

Children learn about Passover, or Pesach, when the Angel of Death "passed over" the homes of the Israelites.

Passover Snacktime

Simple Seder Snacks

Many of the foods traditionally eaten at a *Seder* are discussed in the "Passover Plates" bulletin board activity (p. 38). For an alternative snacktime food during this unit, offer pieces of cracker-like *matzah*, found at many supermarkets, and serve with peanut butter, apple slices, and grape juice.

Passover Game

Color Food Match

Food is fun in this color learning game.

Materials: Food card reproducibles (p. 44) and crayons or markers the colors of the food, or a variety of real or plastic foods of different colors; paper; construction-paper cards the same colors as the foods; scissors

Directions: Copy, color, and cut out a set of the food card reproducibles. On each construction-paper color card, print the name of that card (for example, on a green card print the word "green"). Display the different food cards or real foods. To play the game, show the children a color card. They should match the color of the card with one of the foods on a food card. When a match has been made, the color card and the food card (or cards) should be grouped together. Repeat for each color card. When the game is over, save the food cards and color cards to use another time (laminate for durability). Or glue the cards to a large piece of poster board and display on the wall for children to study again.

EGGING ON EASTER

The Sunday following the first full moon on or after March 21 is the day Christians celebrate Easter and Jesus's resurrection. It is a holiday of great hope because Christians believe it signifies everlasting life. Since the holiday takes place in the spring, Easter is also seen as a time of renewal and growth.

The activities in this unit are accordingly lively and spring-like: children will make fanciful carrots and flowers, sweet bunny baskets to hold delicious candies and decorated eggs, as well as newborn chicks that peek out from behind their opening shells. All of the activities encourage children to have fun in this very special season.

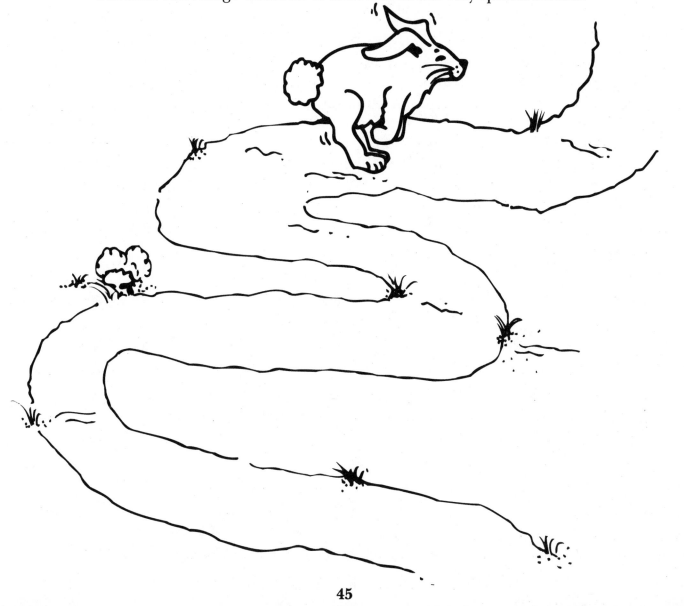

Tree-Riffic Easter Display

Instead of a bulletin board, this display center comes in the shape of a tree. It's fun and easy to put together, and children will love hanging decorated Easter eggs on the tiny branches.

Materials: Table-top tree (store-bought; one you fashion with flower-arranging wire and pastel-colored wrapping paper or colored paper; or a fallen tree branch checked for insects and spray-painted [if desired]); small Styrofoam stand; construction paper (spring colors); scissors; hole punch; nontoxic, washable tempera; shallow paint tray; yarn or ribbon

Directions: Set up your tree. If you are making one, fashion flower-arranging wire into a tree shape and wrap the trunk and branches with paper. Insert the tree trunk (if using wire, double it up) into the Styrofoam stand.

Make a number of decorated Easter eggs by cutting out oval shapes from construction paper. Punch a hole in the top of each paper egg and loop a piece of yarn or festive ribbon through the hole. Tie the yarn ends together. Have the child dip his or her index finger into the paint and make fingerprint dots on one side of each egg. Hang the eggs on the Easter tree to dry. When dry, take the eggs down and have the child make fingerprint imprints on the other side. Hang again. When the unit is over, give the eggs to the child to take home.

decorate eggs and hang

Festive Flower

These construction paper flowers are full of imagination! For a learning activity, save flower seed packages. Then teach children the names of the flowers and show them what the flowers will look like once the seeds have germinated.

Materials: 12" x 18" blue construction paper, pink construction paper (or your choice of flower color), green construction paper, scissors, nontoxic glue, pencil or marker

Directions: For the flower head, trace the child's hand (fingers apart) on pink construction paper. Cut out and set aside. To make leaves, trace the child's hand twice (fingers apart) on green construction paper. Cut out both paper hands and set aside. For the stem, cut a 1" x 18" strip of green construction paper. Fold back and forth so that it looks like a paper accordion.

Now you're ready to put the flower all together. First glue the pink flower to the top of the green stem. Then glue the palm portion of the pink flower (with fingers pointing up and bent slightly forward) to the top of a vertical sheet of blue construction paper (this is the sky). When dry, gently pull the stem down and glue to the bottom of the background. Now slip the paper leaves under both sides of the stem and glue to the background sheet. Curl the fingers forward to give the project a three-dimensional look.

Cheerful Chick

Newborn chicks are cause for a springtime celebration! Children will enjoy this easy-to-make project—and love moving the eggshell back and forth to let the chick peek out!

Materials: White poster board and yellow crayon or yellow construction paper, orange construction paper, scissors, wiggly eyes, paper fastener, pencil, nontoxic glue, transparent or masking tape, hole punch

Directions: To make the eggshell, trace the child's hand (fingers together) on white poster board. Cut out the paper hand and set aside. Make the chick by tracing the child's foot on yellow construction paper (or, for more durability, use white poster board colored with yellow crayon). Cut out the paper foot. Glue wiggly eyes to the heel portion. Add an orange construction paper beak just below the eyes.

Now combine the eggshell and the chick. Position the eggshell so that the paper fingers extend upward. Place the chick directly behind it (with the eyes at the top). Adjust so that the chick's face is at least an inch above the eggshell. Punch a hole through the palm of the eggshell shape and the toe area of the foot. Insert a paper fastener and secure at the back of the chick. Put a piece of tape over any sharp edges. Then let the child have fun with the cheerful chick!

Milk-Bottle Bunny Basket

Here's a project that children and their parents will treasure for more than one Easter holiday. The basket is also a great way to recycle a large plastic milk bottle.

Materials: White or pink construction paper, gallon-size plastic milk bottle, nontoxic glue, pipe cleaners, scissors, wiggly eyes, 1 black and 3 white pompons, stapler and staples, Easter "grass," jelly beans (optional), red felt (optional)

Directions: Cut off the plastic bottle spout (begin cutting by poking a hole with the scissors). Continue cutting off the bottle top, leaving the front of the bottle 4" taller than the back. (The front will be the bunny's face and needs a larger work area.) Cut straight across at the back. Next, glue white pompon eyes with wiggly eyes glued to their center to the front of the bottle. Glue on a black pompon nose and a white bunny tail. Poke a hole on each side of the nose and insert two pipe cleaners for bunny whiskers (the pipe cleaners go in one hole and out the other). Add a smiley red felt mouth if desired.

Now comes the *BodyArt* portion of the project! Trace the child's left and right feet on pink or white construction paper. Cut out the paper feet and glue to the bottom of the milk bottle with the toes sticking out at an angle. To make bunny ears, ask the child to put both palms together. Trace the hands twice (in the vertical position), up to the wrists, on a sheet of pink or white construction paper. Cut out and staple or glue each "ear" to the inside front of the basket. Add Easter grass and jelly beans, and let the child take home the bunny to be admired!

glue ears to bottle

Happy Carrot

This wide-eyed carrot can help you teach a lot about nutrition and the spring. Children can also use it to play the game in this unit (p. 55) and to pretend to feed the milk-bottle bunny they make (p. 49).

Materials: Carrot reproducible (p. 56), scissors, green construction paper, pencil, nontoxic glue, orange crayon or marker, wiggly eyes (optional)

Directions: Copy, color, and cut out the carrot reproducible. Then trace the child's hand (fingers apart) on a sheet of green construction paper. Cut out the paper hand "carrot top." Glue the paper palm to the back of the carrot, with the fingers extending above the carrot. Draw in bright eyes or, if desired, glue on wiggly eyes.

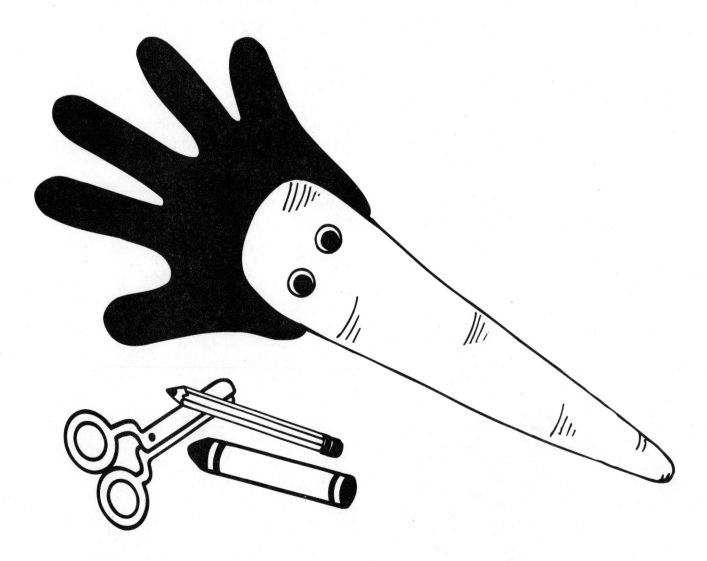

Easter Finger Plays and Movement Songs

Three Things Nice
(to the tune of "Three Blind Mice")

Three things nice,
Three things nice.
What could they be?
What could they be?
Flowers, bunnies, or chicks in a row.
Sunshine, veggies, or birdies, you
    know.
We might as well throw the dice
To choose three things nice!

Ten Little Animals
(to the tune of "Ten Little Indians")

One scratching, two scratching,
    three scratching chickens,
Four scratching, five scratching,
    six scratching chickens,
Seven scratching, eight scratching,
    nine scratching chickens,
Ten scratching chickens all!

(Continue the verses with: hopping
bunnies, mewing kitties, and playing children.)

The Springtime Morning Song

(to the tune of "The Wheels on the Bus")

The chicks in the egg go peck,
    peck, peck,
Peck, peck, peck,
Peck, peck, peck.
The chicks in the egg go peck,
    peck, peck
On a springtime morning.

The bunnies in the field go hop,
    hop, hop,
Hop, hop, hop,
Hop, hop, hop.
The bunnies in the field go hop,
    hop, hop
On a springtime morning.

The carrots in the garden grow,
    grow, grow,
Grow, grow, grow,
Grow, grow, grow.
The carrots in the garden grow,
    grow, grow
On a springtime morning.

The robins in the nest go tweet,
    tweet, tweet,
Tweet, tweet, tweet,
Tweet, tweet, tweet.
The robins in the nest go tweet,
    tweet, tweet
On a springtime morning.

The children at play go yeah, yeah,
    yeah!
Yeah, yeah, yeah!
Yeah, yeah, yeah!
The children at play go yeah, yeah,
    yeah!
On a springtime morning.

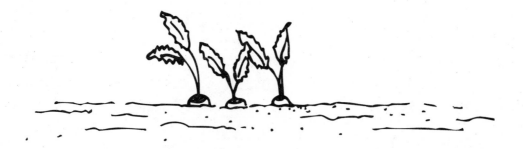

52

Easter Read-Alouds

Fiction

Barrett, John. *The Easter Bear.* Chicago: Children's Press, 1981.

Ted Edward Bear offers his services at Easter when the bunnies go on strike. Fun reading for both children and adults!

Carlson, Nancy. *Bunnies and Their Hobbies.* New York: Puffin, 1984.

After a long, hard day at the office, bunnies like to paint pictures, sunbathe, work in the yard, and work off all those carrots they've eaten! Charming illustrations will entrance the children.

Hopkins, Lee Bennett. *Easter Birds Are Springing.* New York: Harcourt, 1979.

Short, sweet poems that children will enjoy. Illustrations are by Tomie de Paola.

Milhous, Katherine. *The Egg Tree.* New York: Scribner's, 1950.

Katy finds something in her grandma's attic that's very special. This Caldecott Medal winner is a long read-to, but well worth your time.

Rosen, Michael. *Little Rabbit Foo Foo.* New York: Trumpet Club, 1990.

This hilarious Big Book tells of the adventures of the rascally rabbit who keeps scooping up field mice and bopping them on the head, much to the Good Fairy's dismay.

Tafuri, Nancy. *Rabbit's Morning.* New York: Greenwillow, 1985.

A nicely illustrated picture book that teaches such animal names as possum, porcupine, rabbit, and pheasant.

Tresselt, Alvin. *The World in a Candy Egg.* New York: Lothrop, 1967.

Lovely words and pictures tell the story of the community inside a candy egg—one that's spun with sugar and covered with rosebuds high on a shelf in a toy shop.

Nonfiction

Gibbons, Gail. *Easter.* New York: Holiday House, 1989.

A nice explanation of Easter, including the reason why lilies are often on display at that time.

Harland, Jack and John Williams. *The Life Cycle of a Rabbit.* New York: Bookwright, 1988.

Nice big pictures and good information answer lots of questions children have about rabbits.

Heller, Ruth. *Chickens Aren't the Only Ones.* New York: Grosset & Dunlap, 1981.

Ruth Heller's picture books are always wonderfully illustrated, with a story that's informative as well as relevant to young children. This nonfiction book is just as good—a reference for the whole year.

Roser, Wiltrud. *Everything About Easter Rabbits.* New York: Crowell, 1972.

Where does the Easter Rabbit get eggs? Who delivers them? This book will help adults answer questions children ask during this holiday season.

Winthrop, Elizabeth. *He Is Risen—The Easter Story.* New York: Holiday House, 1985.

An adaptation from the New Testament, King James version, that's nicely illustrated for young children.

Easter Snacktime

Veggie Dip

Instead of giving children Easter candy, why not treat them to a springtime veggie dip? The children will love learning about how the planting season yields such delicious food! Whip up your favorite veggie dip and accompany with cut-up raw veggies, such as carrots, cucumbers, beans, and celery. Older children can help cut up softer vegetables with plastic knives. While the children snack, read an Easter- or food-related book to them; later consider taking a field trip to a nearby garden to see where veggies are grown.

Easter Game

Find the Carrot

Here's another way to use the Happy Carrots the children made (p. 50). Just hide one or more of the carrots in the classroom or outside in the playing area. Then let the children find as many as they can. Repeat if there is time and interest.

Note: Put the children's names on the backs of their paper carrots for easy identification after play. Laminate the carrots for durability before hiding them.

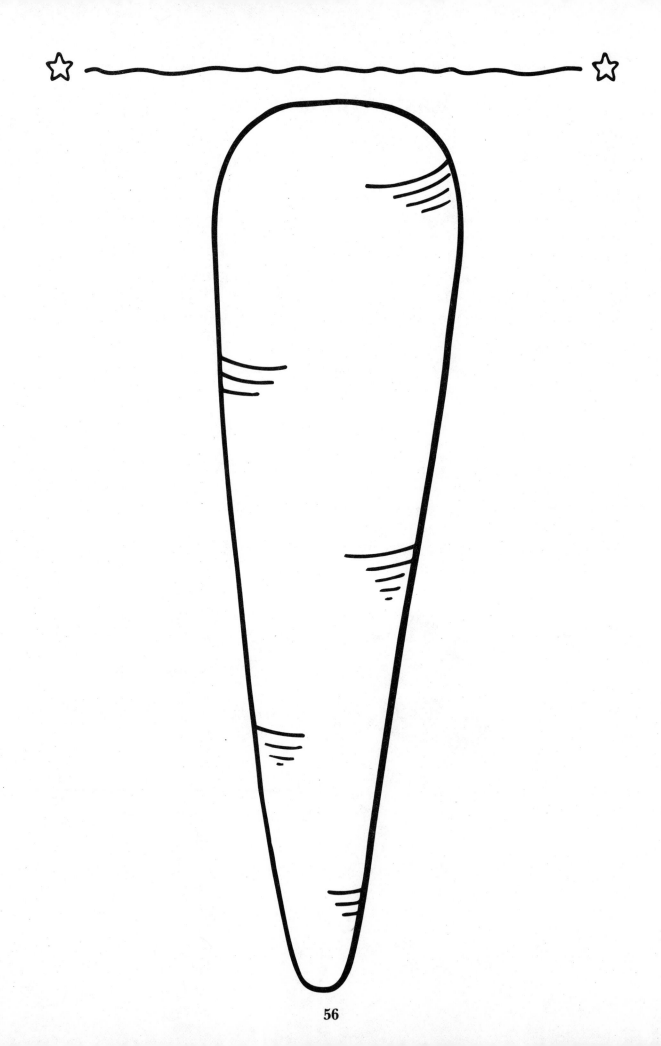

APRIL FOOL'S DAY

April Fool's Day is the name given to the first day of April. It's also known as All Fools' Day. On this very playful day, people play tricks and practical jokes on each other. But the harmless jokes—the ones that give everyone a good laugh—are best!

"Knock, knock" jokes are fun to share on this day. Playing with words is a great way to encourage an appreciation of language. Here's one you might try:

First person—"Knock, knock."
Second person—"Who's there?"
First person—"Don't cha."
Second person— "Don't cha who?"
First person—"Don't cha just love knock, knock jokes?"

What would April Fool's Day be without magic? Magic tricks are also fun to share during this week—with the help of one of this unit's projects you'll be able to pull a rabbit out of a hat!

Clowning around on April Fool's Day is another "must do" activity. Walking in a pair of huge shoes will really get the giggles going. And for those who are always "monkeying around," there's a cute *BodyArt* monkey to create that children are bound to love.

Everything's Coming Up Magic (No Foolin'!) Bulletin Board

Magic and April Fool's Day are perfect companions! That's why the focal point for this celebration is devoted to the illusionary arts. The magic hats in this display hold amazingly long scarves as well as very rascally rabbits!

Materials: Magic hat reproducible (p. 68), nontoxic glue, white poster board, scissors, pencil or marker, construction paper (in several colors), transparent tape

Directions: Copy and cut out six magic hat reproducibles. Glue the six hats onto a large sheet of white poster board. Then cut a 4" slit across each hat's black oval area, cutting through the poster board as well. Make the magically long scarf by tracing 15 to 20 children's hands (fingers together) on a variety of colors of construction paper. Cut out all the hands. Then tape the hands together, fingers to heels, until you have one or more very long strings. Slip one end of a scarf string through the slit in one of the hats. Let the scarf string hang loose or tape it to the poster board (scarves that are loose may be gently pulled out of the hat). Position another scarf string coming out of another hat if you like, but leave several hats open so that some rascally rabbits (see p. 59) can also be pulled out.

Note: Scarf strings don't have to be taped down in straight lines; bends and curves add interest.

glue hands together

cut a 4-inch slit in black oval

Rascally Rabbit

The word "magic" comes from the word "magi," the priests of ancient Persia. This project gives children the chance to learn the difference between tricks in make-believe stories (like the genie coming out of Aladdin's lamp) and the tricks a live magician performs.

Materials: Magician's hat reproducible (p. 68), construction paper (your choice of color), scissors, markers or crayons, pencil, wiggly eyes (optional), glue (optional)

Directions: To make a rascally rabbit, trace the child's hand (fingers apart) on a piece of construction paper. Cut out the entire paper hand. Then cut away the middle finger. The index and ring fingers are the rabbit's ears. The thumb and pinky finger are the rabbit's paws. Bend the paws forward. Then draw in eyes (or glue on wiggly eyes), whiskers, and a sweet little nose on the palm area.

Next, copy and cut out the magician's hat. Make a 4" slit in the black oval area. Slide the rascally rabbit into the magician's hat. Children can take the rabbit home for additional, magical fun.

Note: Add several rascally rabbits to your bulletin board for a hopping good time!

trace hand and bend thumb and pinky forward

add facial features

Clowning Around

It's impossible to frown in clown shoes! Walk a few steps and a smile is bound to break out. And that's what April Fool's Day is all about. Before you begin this activity, tell children a bit about clowns. In ancient times, clowns were called jesters, and their job was to cheer up or amuse the king. Today there are three types of clowns: the Charlie is always in trouble, like Charlie Chaplin; the August wears white makeup and is always falling down; and the Joey is usually an acrobat or juggler.

Materials: Heavy foam board or cardboard, a pair of 36" shoelaces, fabric paint (a color that contrasts with foam board or cardboard), brush, utility knife, pencil or chalk

Directions: To make clown shoes, ask the child to stand (shoes on) on a piece of foam board or cardboard. Trace one shoe. Then trace a similar outline around the first outline, about double the size of the child's actual shoe. Repeat with the other shoe. Cut out both clown-size shoes (an adult should do this). Pick up one and poke a hole on either side of the child's original shoe outline, at the ball of the foot. Loop a shoelace through one hole, across the sole of the clown shoe, and up through the second hole. Repeat for the second shoe.

Using fabric paint, draw clown laces and toes peeking out from under a worn-out shoe (an adult should work with the fabric paint). Repeat for the second clown shoe. When dry, have the child stand on the clown shoes and tie the shoelaces securely in a bow on the top of his or her real shoes. The shoes should be worn to play the "Big Foot" game (p. 66).

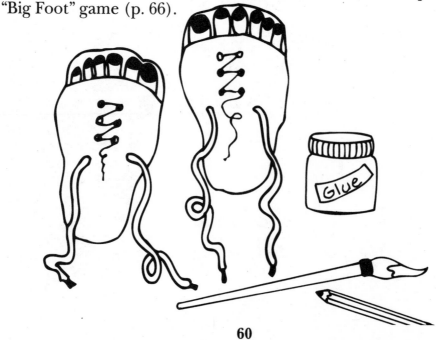

Monkey Business

Monkeys are a favorite with people because they are usually full of tricks and have funny expressions. They're also very resourceful!

Materials: Monkey reproducible (p. 67), scissors, brown crayon, brown construction paper, nontoxic glue, brown cloth tape, Velcro, clear self-adhesive plastic, pencil or marker

Directions: Copy, color (both sides), and cut out the monkey reproducible. Make long, huggable arms by tracing the child's hand (fingers apart) and arm (to the elbow) on a sheet of brown construction paper. Repeat for the other arm. Cut out both paper arms and set aside. Trace the child's foot on a piece of brown construction paper. Repeat for the second foot. Cut out both paper feet.

To attach the arms, secure the base of each arm (at least 1 1/2") to either side of the monkey's back with brown tape. Bend the arms forward. Or, if you wish no tape to show on the monkey's back, cut out a second monkey's back using the original as a guide. Color or use brown construction paper. Tape the monkey's arms as above, but cover with the second back; glue on after the monkey's feet are attached.

Before adding the feet, cover the monkey's body, arms, and feet with clear plastic for durability. Then add a small piece of Velcro to the tip of each paper index finger. Make sure the furry side of one piece is positioned to attach to the sandpapery side of the second piece.

Now add the feet. Tape both paper heels to the back of the base of the body. Bend toes up. If you have decided to "hide" the arm tape with a second back, glue the back on now. Then the child can hug away!

Option: Tape on a long strip of brown paper for a tail.

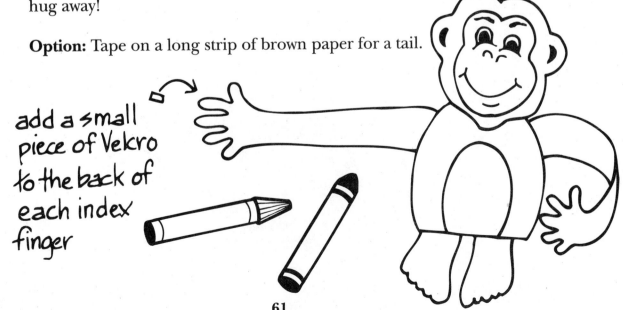

add a small piece of Velcro to the back of each index finger

April Fool's Day Finger Plays and Movement Songs

April Fool's Day Song
(to the tune of "London Bridge")

April Fool's means laughing loud,
Laughing loud, laughing loud.
April Fool's means laughing loud,
My fair children!

April Fool's means jumping high,
Jumping high, jumping high.
April Fool's means jumping high,
My fair children!

April Fool's means running fast,
Running fast, running fast.
April Fool's means running fast,
My fair children!

April Fool's means not being
    fooled,
Not being fooled, not being fooled.
April Fool's means not being
    fooled,
My fair children!

Mr. Magic's Song
(to the tune of "O Christmas Tree")

O magic man, o magic man,
How do you do those tricks?
O magic man, o magic man,
How do you do those tricks?

How do you pull a rabbit
Out of your hat?
O magic man, o magic man,
How do you do those tricks?

April Fool's Finger Play
(to the tune of "Eensy Weensy Spider")

The itsy, bitsy bunny climbed in the
    magic hat.
Down came a hand and grabbed
    him where he sat!
He was so scared he raised his little
    paws
But some people were watching and
    gave him big applause!

April Fool's Day Read-Alouds

Fiction

Allsburg, Chris Van. *Jumanji*. Boston: Houghton Mifflin, 1981.

Jumanji appears to be just a simple board game until a brother and sister start playing while mom and dad are gone.

Amery, Heather. *Rumpelstiltskin*. London: Usborne Publishing, 1988.

This retelling of a traditional fairy tale is especially designed with young listeners and readers in mind. A trick backfires on a little man who has magical powers and a long name.

Anno, Mitsumasa. *Anno's Journey*. New York: Collins World, 1977.

Anno has many imaginative adventures as he visits northern Europe. Also available from Anno: *Anno's Alphabet Counting Book*.

Anno, Mitsumasa. *Topsy-Turvies*. New York: Philomel, 1989.

Anno's pictures stretch the imagination in this wonderfully whimsical story.

Barrett, Judi. *Cloudy with a Chance of Meatballs*. New York: Scholastic, 1978.

Talk about adventures in imagination! When Grandpa's pancake lands on Henry, it reminds Grandpa of the tiny town of Chewandswallow—where food falls from the sky!

Baum, Arline and Joseph. *OPT: An Illusionary Tale*. New York: Puffin Books, 1987.

This exciting story of make-believe takes children on a journey through the kingdom of OPT—short for optical illusions.

Bishop, Claire Huchet and Kurt Wiese. *The Five Chinese Brothers*. New York: Coward-McCann, 1938.

Five identical brothers are able to trick the judge and the village with their special talents.

Brown, Marc. *Arthur's April Fool*. Boston: Little, Brown, 1983.

Everyone is getting ready for April Fool's Day, including Arthur and the town bully, Binky.

Christian, Mary Blount. *April Fool*. New York: Macmillan, 1981.

Seth liked to daydream so much that the adults in the village called him Seth the Dreamer. What happens in this adventurous story with the King of Gotham near Nottingham may very well be how the first April Fool's Day was celebrated.

Dewey, Ariane. *Pecos Bill*. New York: Greenwillow, 1983.

Tall tales are great to read to children on April Fool's Day. In this one, Pecos Bill is saved by coyotes and thinks he is one!

Goode, Diane. *Diane Goode's Book of Silly Stories and Songs.* New York: Dutton, 1992.

Read this book to children during more than one sitting. They'll love the silly stories and songs!

Gould, Deborah. *Terry's Creature.* New York: Lothrop, 1989.

What would happen if something a child drew came to life? Children will find out in this imaginative offering.

Stinson, Kathy. *Those Green Things.* Toronto: Annick Press, 1985.

Mom sees those green things as socks, pyjamas, old clothes, and a garden hose. Her daughter sees them as lizards, giant frogs, and lumpy, bumpy monsters!

Viorst, Judith. *My Mama Says There Aren't Any Zombies, Ghosts, Vampires, Creatures, Demons, Monsters, Fiends, Goblins, or Things.* New York: Aladdin Books, 1973.

Mother sometimes makes mistakes about everyday things, so maybe she's mistaken about the zombies, ghosts, and weird creatures she says aren't real. At least that's what her son worries about!

Yorinks, Arthur. *Hey, Al.* New York: Sunburst, 1986.

Al was dissatisfied with his job, but the paradise he finds isn't what it seems to be in this Caldecott Medal winner, illustrated by Richard Egielski.

Nonfiction

Baker. *April Fools' Day Magic.* Minneapolis: Lerner, 1989.

Magic tricks and April Fool's Day go hand in hand. This magical book shows how to put on a great April Fool's Day celebration!

Churchill, E. Richard and Linda R. *101 Shaggy Dog Stories.* New York: Scholastic, 1975.

Children will love these shaggy dog jokes—don't be surprised if they make up a few of their own!

Gwynne, Fred. *The King Who Rained.* New York: Trumpet Club, 1970.

When daddy says there are forks in the road and mommy says she has a frog in her throat, they don't mean it literally. This fun picture book helps adults understand why children sometimes get confused by what is being said.

Hoban, Tana. *Look! Look! Look!* New York: Scholastic, 1988.

A Big Book in which readers look through a small opening.

Jonas, Ann. *Round Trip.* New York: Mulberry Books, 1983.

Black and white illustrations tell a story that's literally read all around each page! An oldie but goodie that's continually popular with children.

Phillips, Louis. *The Upside Down Riddle Book.* New York: Lothrop, 1982.

Big, bold, abstract closeups of ordinary things make wonderful guessing games for children.

Shaw, Charles G. *It Looked Like Spilt Milk.* New York: Harper Collins, 1947.

Ink spot illustrations reveal a cloud in the sky at book's end. Still readily available in libraries and bookstores.

Supraner, Robyn. *Stop and Look! Illusions.* Mahwah, New Jersey: Troll Associates, 1981.

Some 22 activities you and the children can share during an April Fool's Day celebration. Not every activity is appropriate for young children.

Terban, Marvin. *In a Pickle and Other Funny Idioms.* New York: Clarion, 1983.

The author explains right away that idioms are groups of words that really don't mean what they say, like "butterflies in your stomach." Thirty popular idioms are included in this wonderful book that helps children feel good about language.

Wilson, April. *Look!* New York: Puffin, 1990.

Children get a chance to use their powers of observation to learn about camouflage. Also available: *Look Again!*

April Fool's Day Snacktime

Funny Fruit Salad

To complement the joyful noise of an April Fool's Day celebration, serve a funny fruit salad as a healthy snack. Cut up bananas, peaches, pears, and pineapples (or add your favorite fruit). Then top each serving with a cherry. Mimic different animals eating fruit (monkeys eating bananas, for instance), and watch the smiles spread!

April Fool's Day Game

Big Foot

This learning game teaches children about left and right, counting, and simple directions.

Have all the children put on their clown shoes (see p. 60). Form a line with lots of space in between children. Call out orders, such as "Take two steps forward" or "Take two steps back." The children should follow your directions. When they're comfortable with the game and the required movements, let the children take turns giving orders to the rest of the group. Limit each child to five orders so that everyone has a chance to lead.

CHILDREN'S DAY

Children's Day is a celebration in which the entire world can rejoice, because children are the mortar that binds nations together. Cultures and languages may differ, but love of children is a constant.

Children's Day was first celebrated in 1868 and is now observed annually on the second Sunday in June. Different countries applaud the occasion in various ways, but the holiday is regarded as a happy time to pay homage to our future world leaders.

BodyArt enriches and reinforces this special day's festivities with activities that build self-esteem, help children become more aware of their uniqueness, and show children that friendship is one way to celebrate important relationships.

Let's Hear It for Kids!
Bulletin Board

Being listened to is one way a person can see how much he or she is valued. This bulletin board shows children that they are truly important.

Materials: Ear reproducible (p. 78); 8 ½" x 11" pieces of light-colored paper; markers or crayons; glue; tape; scissors; white poster boards; nontoxic, washable tempera in a variety of skin tones; shallow paint trays

Directions: Interview each child to find out when he or she was born (you may have to consult records for young children), care givers' names, favorite toy, and favorite food. Put this information on an 8 ½" x 11" sheet of light-colored paper horizontally. Title the sheet "All About _____ (insert child's name)." Glue or tape several sheets to as many pieces of poster board as needed. If you wish, angle the sheets to create visual interest, and put a piece of contrasting construction paper behind each sheet to "frame" it. Copy, cut out, and color an ear reproducible for each child and glue one to the right of each interview sheet.

Ask each child to dip one hand (palm side down) into a tray of skin-tone paint. Have the child make one imprint on the poster board immediately beneath his or her interview sheet.

Whole Body Poster

There's nothing like tracing a child's entire body to realize how unique that child really is!

Materials: Markers or crayons, body-size paper (or tape two large poster boards together), scissors, masking tape, pencil

Directions: Have the child lie face up on the paper on the floor and trace his or her head, arms, trunk, and legs. If the child is uncomfortable doing this, simply tape a large piece of paper against a wall and ask the child to stand against the paper to be traced. Once the outline is finished, have the child get carefully off the paper and color in hair, facial features, and clothes. Name the different body parts for reinforcement while coloring is taking place. For additional learning, print the body part words on the back of the outline before rolling up the outline for the child to take home.

Hand Shaker

This fun project encourages children to become aware of other children and of the friendship that can take place between them. The children may use the "Hand Shaker" with the songs on page 74.

Materials: Styrofoam base (saved from packing boxes or bought in a craft store), scissors, construction paper in a variety of skin tones, transparent tape, pipe cleaner, pencil or marker

Directions: Trace the child's hand (fingers slightly apart) on a sheet of construction paper. Cut out the paper hand and set aside. Now wind a pipe cleaner around your finger so that it looks like a tightly coiled spring. Stretch out the pipe cleaner again so that it ends up slightly coiled.

Tape one end of the pipe cleaner to the back of the hand. Push the other end of the pipe cleaner into the Styrofoam base. Now the child can use the "Hand Shaker" to shake hands with other children!

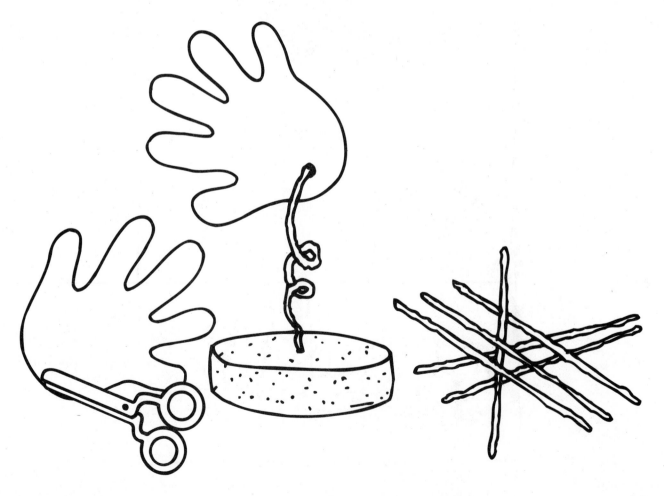

My Gift to You Wrapping Paper

When a child shares something he or she made with another child, a bond is created. Sometimes these bonds of friendship last a lifetime.

Materials: A homemade gift; nontoxic, washable tempera in festive colors; shallow paint trays; white or light-colored 12" x 18" construction paper; transparent tape; ribbon or bow (optional)

Directions: Ask each child to dip a hand (palm down) into a tray of tempera. Have him or her make an imprint on the construction paper. Let the child continue making a design of hand (and finger!) prints using different colors. Set aside the paper to dry.

Meanwhile, have the child create a gift—a drawing is a good idea—for a classmate. If the child doesn't want to give away the drawing, try to make a duplicate so one can be kept and the second given away. Copy machines are godsends when it comes to relieving the minds of young children with regard to this "sharing" principle!

When the wrapping paper is completely dry, place the homemade gift into the center of the undecorated side. Fold up the sides and tape to close. Add a ribbon or bow if desired. Tape a small card to the gift that tells who made it, but leave off the receiver's name. Have the card read "Made Especially for You by _____" (fill in the child's name).

When each child has made and wrapped a gift, set all of the gifts in a prominent place for a period of time (this will build suspense as well as allow children to admire their work). Have an adult distribute the gifts to prevent hurt feelings.

Children's Day Finger Plays and Movement Songs

The Friendship Song

(to the tune of "I've Been Working on the Railroad")

I've been acting like a good friend
All the livelong day.
I've been acting like a good friend
'Cause I want to have a good day.

Can't you hear the laughter
    sounding?
Rise up so early in the morn.
Can't you hear the happy talking?
Be my friend today!

Be my friend today,
Be my friend today,
Can't you, won't you be my friend
    today?
Be my friend today,
Be my friend today,
Won't you be my friend?

Someone's going to be my friend,
A friend I really know, I know.
Someone's going to be my friend,
Is it Luis, Julie, or Joe?

The Sharing Song

(to the tune of "Twinkle, Twinkle, Little Star")

Toys, toys, shining bright,
Fun to play with day or night.
I share with you and you share with
    me.
That's the way for friends to be!

I Like Myself Finger Play

(to the tune of "Are You Sleeping Brother John?")

I like myself, I like myself,
Feet and toes, feet and toes!
Everything about me, everything
    about me
Is one of a kind, one of a kind.

(Add more verses by substituting different body parts, such as arms and legs, eyes and nose, and mouth and ears.)

The Snacktime Song

(to the tune of "On Top of Old Smokey")

We are eating pizza,
It's covered with cheese,
And we will get seconds
If we nicely say please.
Now don't you worry,
There's lots to go 'round.
'Cause we are best friends here,
The best friends we've found!

Children's Day Read-Alouds

Fiction

Aliki. *We Are Best Friends*. New York: Trumpet Club, 1982.

Peter, Robert's best friend, is moving away, and that makes Robert sad. Robert learns, however, that he can have more than one friend when a new boy named Will moves into the neighborhood.

Jabar, Cynthia. *Party Day!* Boston: Little, Brown, 1987.

This birthday counting book makes learning fun for young readers.

Krauss, Ruth. *Big and Little*. New York: Scholastic, 1987.

Young children fall in love with this picture book because it gives them lots of good feelings about being little.

Schwartz, Amy. *Bea and Mr. Jones*. New York: Puffin Books, 1983.

Bea and her dad, Mr. Jones, switch "jobs" and find out that children do as well in the business world as adults do in kindergarten!

Viorst, Judith. *Alexander and the Terrible, Horrible, No Good, Very Bad Day*. New York: Aladdin Books, 1972.

Alexander is a lively little boy who is definitely having a bad day. Fortunately his mom convinces him that moving to Australia is not the answer.

Viorst, Judith. *Alexander, Who Used to Be Rich Last Sunday*. New York: Macmillan, 1978.

Alexander used to be rich, but now he has only bus tokens—all because he made some unwise choices about money management. Even young children appreciate Alexander's woeful predicament.

Viorst, Judith. *The Tenth Good Thing About Barney*. New York: Macmillan, 1971.

When Barney the cat dies, the boy who took care of him tries to think of 10 good things to say at the cat's funeral. A sensitive look at children and their pets.

Wood, Audrey. *Quick As a Cricket*. Singapore: Child's Play, 1989.

This book helps children feel good about themselves by helping them accept all dimensions of their personality. Comparisons between a child and an animal help instill the love of words as well as prepare the way for learning about similes and metaphors.

Zolotow, Charlotte. *I Like to be Little*. New York: Harper and Row, 1966.

Most children want to be big like their parents or adult care givers. In this book, however, the little girl likes being little and finds many things she can do because of her size.

Nonfiction

Aliki. *Feelings*. New York: Mulberry Books, 1984.

Comic-strip illustrations show children all the feelings they may have —from happy to sad to loud to quiet. Having different feelings is all part of being a child.

Aliki. *My Five Senses*. New York: HarperCollins, 1989.

Children not only learn the names of the five senses, but also how they are used to perform even simple acts.

Cauley, Lorinda Bryan. *Clap Your Hands*. New York: Scholastic, 1992.

In this book, children learn many of the neat things they can do with their body—from roaring like a lion to rubbing their tummies.

Fantini, Leo. *My Tooth Came Out Yesterday*. North Billenica, Mass.: Curriculum Associates, 1991.

Lots of different changes take place when a tooth falls out. This Big Book tells how the mouth feels when a tooth is missing.

Fox, Mem. *Time for Bed*. San Diego: Harcourt Brace, 1993.

A beautifully illustrated picture book that is bound to be a favorite.

Rankin, Laura. *The Handmade Alphabet*. New York: Scholastic, 1991.

A "Reading Rainbow" featured book, this offering informs children about sign language in a way they can understand and appreciate.

Whitfield, Dr. Philip and Dr. Ruth. *Why Do Our Bodies Stop Growing?* New York: Viking Kestrel, 1988.

Why do we have to eat so many different kinds of food? Why do ears pop in an airplane? These and other questions are addressed in this informative resource.

Yolen, Jan. *Hands*. Littleton, Mass.: Sundance, 1976.

This delightful nonfiction offering tells how hands are used to make life easier and to express feelings. A good book to have for each child.

Children's Day Snacktime

Cheese Pizza Pies

Children love cheese pizza and sharing one is a great way to show them that each piece contributes to a whole. When children are friends and do things together, anything is possible!

Buy a frozen pizza, have a fresh one delivered from your local pizza parlor, or create one of your own using a favorite recipe. Making one is a bit messy, but you can use ingredients that make the snack a healthy one. After sharing the pizza and cleaning up, have an adult distribute small gifts to the children to reinforce the idea that friendship and sharing are important.

Children's Day Game

My Body Matching Game

Materials: Body parts reproducibles (pp. 79-80), scissors, crayons or markers, self-adhesive plastic coating (optional), #10 envelope

Directions: Copy, cut out, and color the reproducibles twice for a group game. Laminate the game pieces for durability if desired. Store the pieces in an envelope. To play, turn both sets of pieces over so that no pictures are showing. Then have children take turns trying to choose two matching pieces. When a match is made, it is taken off the board. Continue playing until all pieces match and are taken off the board. Play again as long as interest is high. Make additional copies of game pieces for children to take home to play with.

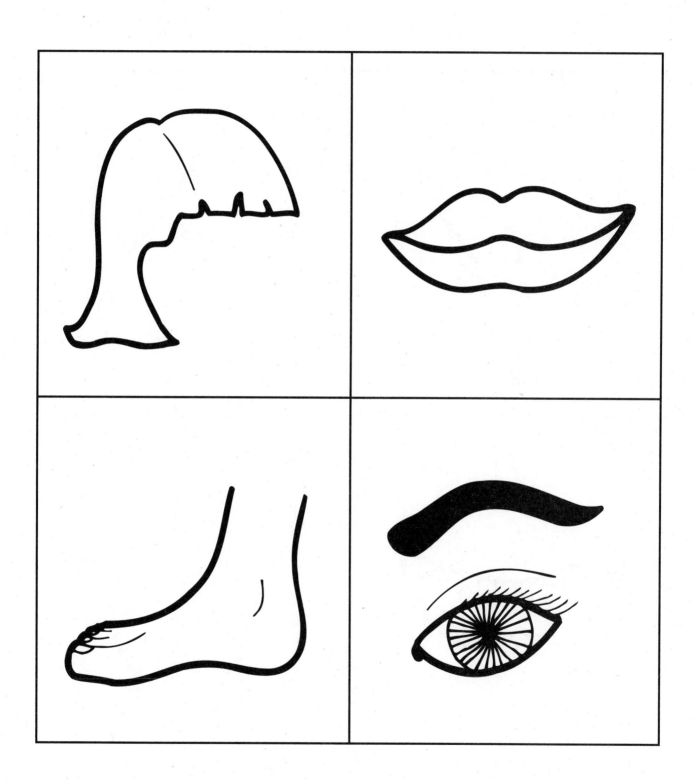

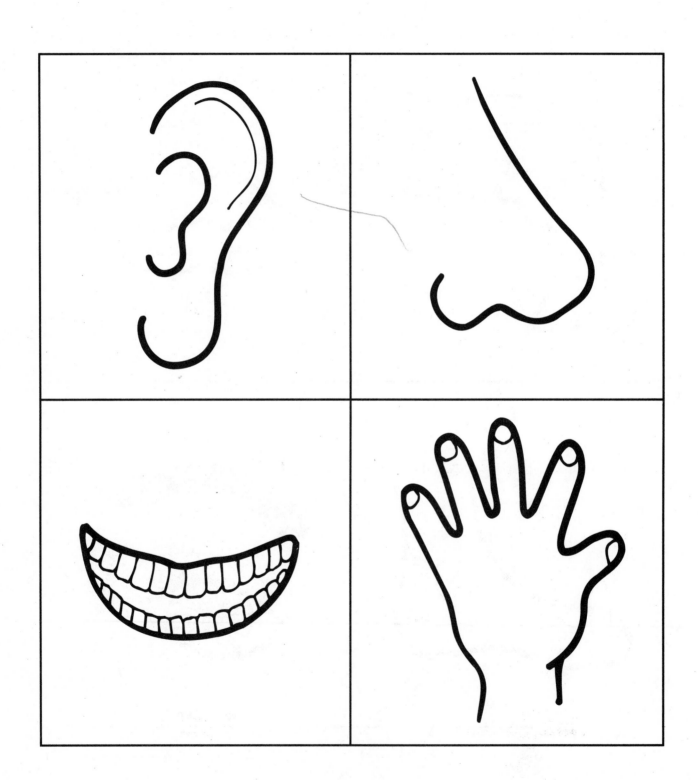